The World's Great Ghost and Poltergeist Stories

The World's Great Ghost and Poltergeist Stories

by
Sarah Hapgood

foulsham
LONDON . NEW YORK . TORONTO . SYDNEY

foulsham
The Publishing House, Bennetts Close,
Cippenham, Berkshire SL1 5AP

ISBN 0-572-02049-X

Printed in Great Britain by
St Edmundsbury Press Ltd, Bury St Edmunds, Suffolk

Contents

Europe

North America

Asia

Africa

Australia

South America

Introduction

Like jokes, themes for stories, and excuses for murder, the paranormal has only a few original bases from which it all springs. On reading through all the cases gathered in this volume, it would seem that each example could be neatly slotted into one or the other of the following definitions: apparitions, disembodied noises, ghost lights, poltergeists, religious phenomena, spontaneous combustion, and stone showers. But because the paranormal is a far from logical subject, this means that each case does not stay quietly in its own box, instead they leap about from one to the other in a frantic fashion. One thing they do have in common though, is the fact that each and every one of these seven categories can occur absolutely anywhere. The following is a brief summary of the sort of phenomena experienced.

1: APPARITIONS

Probably the most romantic form of supernatural phenomena, mainly because they never seem to harm anyone. They are like video recordings of another time superimposed on our present, which dissolve quickly when we try to tamper with them. They range from the mundane to the bizarre. People all over the world have seen them as aliens from outer space to Indian goddesses come to life, whilst many just accept them as part of everyday life . On the whole these spectres tend to ignore us entirely, but that doesn't mean that their presence need not be very unnerving, a gentleman in Australia for example packed up and moved out of his house when he saw a spooky-looking phantom staring out of his living-room window. They have also been known to pop up at random on photographs, when the happy snapper had unwittingly taken a picture of an image from the past.

The knowledge that apparitions are images from a bygone age, unaware of our presence, could be very reassuring for the apprehensive ghost-hunter, if it wasn't for cases such as that of the deceased artist, Meri Genetz, who haunts her old flat in Helsinki. What strange mix-up in physics is it that enables a ghost from the past to engage in conversation with a living person? Such cases are still very rare though, and most witnesses fail to gain a spark of recognition out of the apparition they have seen. Apparitions are the most elusive form of supernatural phenomena. Even when dates and times of day are available for a regular sighting, it is often disappointing to go looking for them. As many eager publicans with a ghost in-situ will tell you, apparitions cannot be summoned to appear at a particular time. Until we know exactly what kind of conditions are needed to generate a ghostly appearance, such information is not of the value we would like it to be.

It should not be forgotten that apparitions can also be images of people who are still alive. Dying people for instance have been known to project visions of themselves to loved ones on the other side of the world. Ghostly phenomena on occasions manifests itself around people who are about to depart this world, as though there was a sudden surge in psychic discharge from the person involved. The creation of apparitions of normal healthy living people has been known to be purely accidental on the part of the protagonist, who often has no idea that their doppelganger is masquerading as themselves in another place from their physical body. This is another slant on out-of-body experiences, and astral projection. There is often no apparent reason whatsoever why a doppelganger should suddenly appear. The person whose image is projected may not even be in the thoughts of the witness who sees it. The claim of astral projection does rather promote the idea that humans are capable of being in two places at once.

There are also rare instances of apparitions being sighted in poltergeist outbreaks, which could imply that poltergeist phenomena is not purely a product of the human subconscious, as I believe it is in the majority of cases. It would seem that apparitions could be either an image from the past superimposed on the present, the product of a person's subconscious appearing to other receptive people, or that old favourite, an entity from beyond the grave. My own favourite theory is that perhaps different time dimensions exist side-by-side, like grooves on a long-playing record, and occasionally overlap. This would explain the many cases we have of buildings and landscapes from another time appearing to a witness. It would also explain cases of communicating apparitions, like Meri Genetz or the numerous cases of phantom hitch-hikers the world over. This opens up the tantalising idea that perhaps some images of people, buildings and landscapes that are seen ... may be of the future.

2: DISEMBODIED NOISES

If we think of supernatural phenomena as being like a battery that runs down over several years, then we can see how a haunting, which may have started out as quite impressive at one time, can be reduced to merely the odd desultory footstep etc. There are numerous cases of inhabitants of houses who may not believe their home is haunted in the conventional spooky sense, but who may hear noises from time to time that are unaccountable. It could be that they are unwittingly catching the very tail-end of a haunting, which is spurting out now and again as though it is using up its very last vestiges of power.

Sometimes ghostly noises are not heard by the human ear, and can only be sensed by animals, or in some cases tape-recorders, as in the case of the haunting of the Point Lookout Lighthouse, Maryland, USA. Voices recorded by psychic investigators there, pinpointed the haunting as belonging to the American Civil War period, when a field hospital stood in the area. The voices were indecipherable, but when replayed on tape they became as clear as a bell. This sort of phenomenon is indicating that the haunting is slowly fading, the way that a cassette tape would after several years of use. But because of this be very wary of people who will tell you that their resident ghost has haunted the area for nearly a 1000 years and is still going strong. English pubs are particularly fond of that old yarn.

A haunting that dates back to an incident centuries before, may now only manifest itself in the odd noise now and again, apparitions that appear colourless and silent like a photographic negative, or balls of light which can often be seen over the sites of old battlefields. Which leads us neatly into the next category.

3: GHOST LIGHTS

Ghost lights, or spook lights as they are known in the States, are phosphorous balls of light that can usually be seen bobbing around an area over several years. Very often they are ball lightning, or balls of methane rising from marshland. They have a long-standing place in folklore all over the world, and each country has had its own meaning to them in the past. In Ireland they were believed to be evil spirits and children were warned to wear their clothes inside out if they were caught outside after dark, in order not to be lured away by them. The Swedish believed they were the souls of unbaptised babies. In Africa it was believed to be 'witch-fire', sent by witches to warn sinners to clean up their acts. The USA has hundreds of cases of ghost lights, usually in the Appalachian mountains, where they were sometimes believed to indicate where treasure was buried. They are also seen around railway tracks, and many American ghost stories interpret the spook lights as a decapitated railwayman with a bobbing lantern, eternally looking for his head! Out of all supernatural phenomena this one is probably the most easily explainable, as in most cases it is obvious that it is a natural phenomenon. Nowadays though ghost lights tend to get mixed up more with UFO phenomena than anything supernatural, but in the realm of the Unexplained the line between supernatural phenomena and UFO phenomena is becoming more and more blurred. This is becoming especially apparent where poltergeists are concerned.

4: POLTERGEISTS

Poltergeist activity is probably the most terrifying form of supernatural phenomena. It is often uncontrollable, as many priests, witch-doctors and mediums the world over have found, and people have been bitten and punched, had their furniture burned and wrecked, lost their homes, and in some rare cases, been seriously injured, through contact with these noisy spirits, or even worse, see the Jabuticabal Poltergeist in Brazil, in which it seems, a young girl was possibly driven to taking her own life.

When a poltergeist invades a home, objects may be moved, doors slam, outbreaks of rapping occur on the walls, and in some more distinguished cases inexplicable outbreaks of fire, and water, oil, or even human blood spurting from the wall in great quantities have been experienced. But bear in mind that poltergeist activity is linked to people not places. If a home is suddenly and inexplicably bombarded with this violent phenomenon, remember it is not the house that is the catalyst, it is usually one of the inhabitants or someone closely associated with the building. Because of this it has always been relatively easy for the sceptics to denounce poltergeists as purely the work of attention-seeking fraudsters.

Some physical mediums, psychics or sensitives, (Uri Geller is a famous example) can move objects, it is claimed, purely by exerting the power of their subconscious, and it is this incredible energy, known as psycho-kinesis, that can create poltergeist activity, when it is unharnessed and unknown to the catalyst involved. Poltergeist epicentres or catalysts tend to be adolescent children, (as in a famous poltergeist outbreak of recent times, the Enfield haunting, where the catalyst, a 12-

year-old girl, was experiencing menstruation for the first time), but they have also been invalids, terminally ill people, those who are chronically frustrated sexually and anyone going through a severe crisis of conscience about their religious faith, or just suffering from severe stress. All these people have one thing in common in that they are mentally confused, frustrated, or deeply unhappy and unsatisfied. People have moved house to get away from their poltergeist but this would not make much difference if the catalyst moves with them, unless of course the catalyst wanted to move all along.

The majority of poltergeist outbreaks tend to last for three or four months, but there have been some cases that have lasted from a mere day or two, to ones that have rumbled on for several years. The phenomena usually dies away when there is an improvement in the life style of the affected family. It is an interesting fact that in the northern hemisphere a lot of poltergeist outbreaks occur during the autumn and winter months, and it has led me to speculate whether it could have anything to do with the illness known as S.A.D., Seasonal Affective Disorder, a debilitating sickness that is now medically recognised.

Another aspect could be the onset of the stressful period of Christmas. But a number of cases continue when the dark months are over and, unfortunately we cannot simply pigeonhole all poltergeist outbreaks as being purely psychological. In past centuries any catalyst suffering at the centre of a poltergeist outbreak was dubbed as being the victim of demonic possession, and dreadful exorcisms were usually performed, with varying degrees of success. Even in these enlightened times some people cannot rule out the evil spirit syndrome, believing that a catalyst may sometimes serve as a suitable foil for an earthbound spirit, and that is when we have those poltergeist cases where vague apparitions are seen, or automatic writing is experienced. In a Gloucestershire poltergeist outbreak in the early 1960s it was claimed that a 14-year-old boy was the catalyst for an entity, who turned out to be one of the builders of the house who had died several years before.

A purported entity may use the catalyst to make its presence felt and not realising it is dead, may become frustrated, throwing furniture about for example. It will use ploys like that to get attention from the inhabitants of the house, rather like an unhappy youngster throwing a tantrum to get affection and recognition. Treating the poltergeist as you would a petulant child is often a propitious approach. It is not unusual for families to get used to a poltergeist in their midst and accept it as part of everyday life, but personally, I do not think this is a good idea. The inconvenience the phenomena creates can produce considerable frustration and unhappiness in a house, hence the old superstition that some homes become 'unlucky'. Very often inhabitants of such houses find that little will go right for them until help is sought for, in my opinion, houses absorb atmospheres like sponges and poltergeists create very negative atmospheres, especially concerning masses of energy which is being totally misdirected by the catalyst for entirely negative results. Sometimes the catalyst tries to keep the phenomena going long past its shelf life because they are enjoying the attention being obtained. This is indeed an unhealthy lifestyle for a child. There is no magic formula for cleaning a house of its poltergeist. Sometimes a priest performing a religious exorcism can work, sometimes it doesn't. Likewise with mediums. There is even a growing band of New Age exorcists who perform non-Christian rites. Sometimes an improvement or understanding of the catalyst's problems can help, although this does get harder the longer the phenomena is allowed to flourish unchecked. Sometimes it will exhaust itself, depending on how strong the problems are, whilst on occasions a completely eccentric solution is found, as in the Pontefract poltergeist who was extinguished by hanging garlic around the house! One Richmond victim achieved an 'instant exorcism' by swearing at what he thought to be a 'poltergeist entity'.

The longer an outbreak is allowed to go on, the harder the problem becomes to deal with. The catalyst, as in the Enfield case, may be used to being the centre of attention and will go all out to keep it going, embellishing the 'poltergeist's pranks'. The arguments will rumble on for years, with sceptics using the dubious character of the catalyst to denounce the whole thing. The Enfield case is also a prime example of how naive some psychic investigators can be, for when the catalyst started growling obscene words, the investigator believed it had to be the entity speaking as no 'nice young girl' would know such words!

5: RELIGIOUS PHENOMENA

Much religious phenomena can be classified under the umbrella of poltergeist activity. On a regular occurrence in most countries in the world some form of unexplained phenomena, with a heavy religious association, takes place. They tend to vary very little, statues and pictures bleed or weep, or witnesses hear messages and miracle cures take place. I am reluctant to say it is, in my opinion, all purely psychological because that makes it sound like mass hysteria, but I am afraid that that is what it appears to be. The weeping statues and bleeding pictures are too similar to those poltergeist cases in which walls drip blood etc, to be discounted. I do not doubt for one minute that the witnesses to the religious phenomena are genuine in their beliefs, but in many ways it is their fervent faith that is triggering the events. Mass hysteria cannot be ruled out either. To illustrate this point, we have the case of the Knock shrine in Ireland, where the statue of the Virgin Mary, is said to move. Millions of devout Catholics flock there every year, probably all desperately yearning for some sign from God. Ireland is prolific in religious phenomena, and on a visit there it is easy to see why. Shrines and Virgin Marys' line the roadsides everywhere, and many Irish Catholics still cross themselves reverently when passing a church. One person's enthusiasm only has to get the better of them for everyone to believe what they think they see. This isn't to underestimate the effect that these mass hallucinations can have. For well over a century Lourdes in France has been a mecca for people seeking miracle cures, and all because one adolescent French girl called Bernadette, who was hungry, over-worked and frail, hallucinated that she saw an image of the Virgin Mary promising her a better life somewhere else.

6: Spontaneous Combustion

Inexplicable outbreaks of fire are a fairly common occurrence in poltergeist activity, where household objects, clothes and furniture can ignite at random with no warning. This leads me to the cause of death which still has the medical experts baffled to this day, Spontaneous Human Combustion.

Cases of people bursting into flames are numerous.

People have spontaneously combusted whilst dancing, sitting in cars or sleeping in bed, and in all cases their whole bodies have burnt to a crisp, whilst anything nearby has remained unscorched. Theories of the sceptics that the victims sat too close to their electric fire, or set fire to themselves whilst smoking, do not hold water when each case is put under the microscope.

The earliest recorded case occurred in Paris in 1673, and since then there has been a steady line of human fireballs, with victims ranging from aged alcoholics to a four month old baby sleeping in his cot. Spontaneous Human Combustion rarely varies in how it occurs, in that the heat of the flames is usually as intense as that of a crematorium, and yet the victims appear to feel no pain, some in fact are even unaware that they are burning. At the turn of the century in England a servant-girl was casually sweeping the floor at a farmhouse whilst flames shot out of her back! In a lot of cases the fire seems to start in the victim's chest or abdomen and then burns rapidly outwards.

In past centuries, SHC was regarded as some kind of Biblical vengeance, but nowadays there are numerous theories expounded to try and explain the mystery. None of which have been proved. Yet my own favourite is the theory of Psychic Heat. Tibetan monks train themselves diligently in the art of mind over matter. They discipline their subconscious to such an extent that they can sit naked outside in freezing temperatures, and yet train the deepest parts of their minds to heat their bodies. Undertakers, when embalming corpses, often notice that burn marks appear on the flesh of the well-nourished ones. This can happen to those who are still alive as well. There is a case of a Canadian woman who woke up after a four hour sleep to find burn marks on her thighs and abdomen. What if the victims of SHC were unaware of, and thus unable to control, the psychic heat that may have been surging through their bodies, thus resulting in their injury, or often death? Even more baffling are cases where the victim can cause electrical items to fail and other things to burn just by being around them.

The world is made up of electrical force-fields, some of which may generate poltergeist phenomena. In many hauntings it is not unusual for televisions to burn out, lights to flick on and off, and other household gadgets to play up. Again we cross into the UFO area here. During the extensive UFO activity around Broadhaven, Wales, in 1977, which centered on a remote farmhouse, the inhabitants were plagued by televisions and cars burning out, and experienced much phenomena we normally associate with a haunting. The phenomena seemed to centre on the farmer's wife, and diminished when she wasn't around. Are UFO investigators barking up the wrong tree entirely by looking for extraterrestrials? Is much of the phenomena really more in the poltergeist field?

I haven't included any cases of death by SHC in this book because it is a complex subject but there are books on the market dealing solely with SHC and they should be consulted for a full view of this intriguing and frightening phenomenon.

7: STONE SHOWERS

When poltergeist activity breaks out sometimes the building itself is pelted with bricks, stones and sundry other bits of rubble. Stone showers can rain down out of a cloudless sky, and are one of the most inexplicable forms of poltergeist phenomena. In most cases people are not hurt and property remains undamaged, and yet this isn't always the case, for in some instances considerable damage has been caused. Single buildings aren't always the targets either, sometimes whole streets or even small towns have been affected.

Stone showers could be associated with the more bizarre forms of natural phenomena, such as fish falls etc, if it wasn't for that mysterious fact that stone showers rarely cause damage, and people struck by the rubble have been unhurt. Stone showers have also been known to occur in locked rooms. One of the most inexplicable instances of stone showers occurred in 1983 in the Arizona desert, when for three months showers of stones rained down on a house every evening from precisely 5.30 until 7.00 p.m. It is rare for any other form of falling missile to be so accurate in its timing! We cannot rule out a poltergeist connection with stone showers, and the force field factor is very strong here.

Many areas where hauntings occur and there is concentrated UFO phenomena, are often found to be where ley lines cross. Ley lines are supposed to be invisible energy routes in straight lines, which connect ancient and mystical locations, like Stonehenge or old churches built on pagan sites. They are said to carry intense power which our ancestors knew about, and built their sacred sites in particular spots for that reason. Some call them 'flying saucer runways', as Ufologists believe that the leys are used by UFOs as guiding lines. Concentrated UFO phenomena and hauntings are often found to take place on nodes, the points where the lines cross. The farm in the Broadhaven case stands on a node, as does the church in Borley which is still claimed to be in the most haunted village in the world.

Even disregarding extraterrestrial visitors, the ley lines are still thought to be of great importance in psychic research, where unlocking the secrets of their intense energy may lead to the greatest clues in unravelling the whole mystery of ghosts and hauntings.

The field of the Unexplained is a vast one, encompassing many complex and mind-boggling areas, and yet the subject of ghosts is the one that has baffled mankind since he first walked this Earth. The Unexplained has its fads and fashions, and yet ghosts and hauntings have remained constant. It is a subject which has completely refused to go away.

Even in these cynical times, where in a logical world science would have explained it all by now, a high ratio of the world's population believes in ghosts. A vast amount of people claim to have had a supernatural experience of one kind or another, over 80 per cent in a recent survey, from those who have actually lived in a haunted house, to those who have simply had an experience they cannot explain. Even if nine out of ten cases were to have a perfectly rational explanation, there still leaves that small minority that cannot be defined. Ghosts form a part of every culture on this Earth. They have a special place in the human psyche. To deny their existence would be an act of folly and to indicate a lack of tolerance, understanding and knowledge.

SAMUEL WESLEY'S HAUNTED HOUSE

December 1719/January 1720
Epworth Rectory, Lincolnshire, England

The Wesleys didn't have an easy time of things here. Samuel's daughter Hetty described the local village of Wroot as a 'place devoid of wisdom, wit or grace'. In return the villagers didn't think much of the Wesleys, and in 1709 burnt down the rectory and maimed the cattle as a protest at the Rev. Wesley's beliefs. The house was rebuilt. The Rev. Wesley's marriage was also constantly under strain. On one occasion he left his wife because she wouldn't say a prayer for King William III. His wife said she couldn't because she didn't believe a Prince of Orange should be on the English throne. The Rev. Wesley, a bit of a prig at the best of times, left home for a year and returned most reluctantly.

Hardly surprising, with all this hostility in the house, that poltergeist activity broke out on 1 December 1719. Groaning noises were heard from the dining-room, a hand-mill was seen turning by itself and a stamping noise, as though someone was walking around in jackboots, was heard. At night footsteps were heard on the stairs, as well as the sound of dancing and door-latches rattling. Eventually knocking broke out in the Rev. Wesley's bedroom. The noises always began regularly every night at 9.45. Mrs Wesley thought the noises were due to rats and ordered a horn to be sounded to drive them away. From them on the ghostly noises were heard during the day as well.

The children nicknamed the ghost 'Old Jeffrey' and one, Emilia, thought it was a result of local witchcraft. Curiously Hetty Wesley was the only member of the family to sleep through the disturbances each time. The Rev. ordered the spirit to confront him in his study, but when he tried to reach the room the door was pushed shut against him. During prayer sessions, if the Rev. Wesley ordered prayers to be said for the King, the poltergeist would rap angrily, displaying anti-Hanoverian tendencies. Not an uncommon thing at the time! Phantom rabbits and badgers were also seen in the house. Everyone urged the Rev. to move, but he said he wouldn't be driven out by the devil. Suddenly at the end of January the haunting ceased completely.

THE AVENGING GHOST
1730s
Devon, England

George Harris was at the court of King George II in London when he received a message asking him to return home as soon as he could. His butler, Richard Morris, had been disturbed in the night by intruders breaking into the butler's pantry. When he accosted them he found two roughnecks and Richard Tarwell, a 14-year-old boy who had recently been hired as a kitchen help. They tied Morris up and fled. Silver had gone missing. A few nights later George woke to find Tarwell in his room. He was rather surprised as he had personally locked the house up himself before retiring. It was only when Tarwell made no noise that he realised he was seeing a ghost.

Tarwell beckoned him to follow him and they went downstairs. He led him into the grounds and took him to an oak tree where he pointed at the ground and vanished. The next morning Harris and two footmen dug at the spot and found Tarwell's decomposing body. Morris broke down and confessed that he had let the robbers in, as they were his accomplices. Tarwell had caught them stealing the silver and they had killed him. Morris was hung for his crime.

THE COCK LANE GHOST
November 1759/1862
Cock Lane, Smithfield, London, England

The house of Richard Parsons was inflicted by the most famous ghost of the 18th century,a ghost known rather unfortunately at the time as "Scratching Fanny". One night Fanny Lynes, who was lodging at the house, was sharing a room with Elizabeth, Richard's ten year old daughter. Suddenly both heard scratching and rapping noises. Richard thought it was probably the cobbler working in the house next door but soon after Fanny contracted smallpox and died in a house nearby on 2 February 1760. She was six months pregnant at the time. The knocking in Richard Parson's house grew louder, and seemed to centre behind young Elizabeth's bed. Richard called in a carpenter to rip out the walls to find the cause for the knocking sounds, but nothing was found.

Finally, Richard called in the Rev. John Moore, vicar of the nearby church of St Sepulchres. Moore communicated with the spirit, and said it was the ghost of Fanny Lynes, who claimed that she had been poisoned by her common-law husband, William Kent. Richard was delighted at this news as there was no love lost between him and Kent. He had borrowed money off Kent at one time but had failed to pay it back, because he had a drink problem that swallowed everything he earned. He had been hoping to get out of the debt by using William and Fanny's non-marital status as a basis for blackmail. If the entity was Fanny though, this didn't take into account the fact that the rappings had started whilst she was still alive, and that a local publican, called Franzen, had seen an apparition in the area in December 1759, two months before Fanny died.

In despair Kent sought out the Rev. Moore's help as well and a seance was held in Elizabeth's bedroom but to Kent's horror the same scurrilous story was repeated. "Thou art a lying spirit!" Kent wailed. The effects of the haunting began to spread all over London. People even went to listen by Fanny's grave, in case any knockings broke out there. Elizabeth was staying at a friend's house in Cow Lane when a loose curtain began to spin on its rod and the following day Richard heard whispering noises coming from his daughter's bed, even though she was fast asleep and her mouth was closed. The noises became so loud that their host asked them to leave.

They couldn't go back home, as it was still crowded with sightseers (Richard was quite happy to charge an entrance fee to visitors so that they could come into the house and see the site of the weird knockings) so they went to stay at another friend's house in Covent Garden. A desperate Kent told Elizabeth that if she failed to produce the ghost that night her father would be thrown into prison. In panic Elizabeth took a small piece of wood to bed with her and started knocking on it. The board was discovered and the whole thing was denounced as a fraud. Parsons was found guilty of trying to get Kent illegally charged with murder and was sentenced to two years in prison and three stints in the pillory. The Rev. Moore was given a substantial fine for his part in the 'fraud'.

Public opinion was firmly behind Parsons though, and a collection was started for him. Nonetheless the Cock Lane Ghost became synonymous with fraud for centuries after. It's only now that we can look at the case, and by comparing it with other similar hauntings, realise it probably was genuine poltergeist activity, and that, like many hauntings, it was muddled by the dubious characters of the people involved. The centre of the haunting was undoubtedly Elizabeth, and there is one theory that she may have had a crush on William Kent, and this, combined with the onset of puberty and sexual awareness, caused the rappings to start around her bed.

LORD LYTTELTON'S VISION OF DOOM

November 1779

Mayfair, London, England and Dartford, Kent, England

Dr Samuel Johnson was quite impressed with this case and described it as "extraordinary". It certainly was that. On 24 November 1779 Lord Lyttelton, 35, had just returned from Ireland and was staying at his Mayfair home. He had a houseful of guests that night, including two of his mistresses. He was woken later by a fluttering of wings and on drawing back the curtains around his bed, was confronted by a tall figure in white who warned him that he would die in three days! Not surprisingly Lord Lyttelton was taken aback by this and yelled for a servant, who found him in a considerable agitated state. By the next evening he was feeling better though, and told his guests that there was nothing to worry about and invited them to his country house, Pitt Place in Surrey, for the weekend.

On Sunday morning he was boasting that if he survived the night he would have beaten the ghost. That night he retired at 11 o'clock, although this is difficult to verify as some of his guests claimed to have tampered with the clock to make him feel better. Soon after he had a convulsive fit and died. A short while later Miles Andrews, a close friend of Lytteltons and MP for Bewdley, was having a party at his Dartford home but feeling unwell, he went to bed early. Suddenly the curtains on his bed were pulled back and the figure of Lord Lyttelton was standing there in his nightclothes.

"It's all over for me, Andrews", he said in a depressed voice before disappearing. How right he was.

THE BEALINGS BELL-RINGER

2 February/27 March 1834

Great Bealings, Suffolk, England

The Georgian home of Major Edward Moore was disturbed on 2 February when all the service bells suddenly rang out at once. They were to continue to do so, at random, for the following few weeks. Major

Moore was fascinated by the phenomenon, and wrote to the papers asking for help on his mysterious bell-ringer. The bells would usually ring about three times between the hours of 2 and 5 o'clock in the afternoon. Major Moore heard it himself several times, but it was most commonly heard by the servants. Once Moore was standing in the kitchen when the bells began to ring so violently that he thought they would come away from their moorings. That evening the bells rang again whilst he and his son were having dinner.

On another occasion the bells rang so aggressively that one hit the ceiling. The phenomenon ceased as suddenly as it had started, on 27 March.

THE LADY IN WHITE
July 1837
Blandford, Dorset, England

Three year old Polly Allen came running into the house one day to tell her mother that she had seen a tall woman in white walking down the hill opposite their home. Her mother thought she was talking nonsense as no woman would be wearing white on a normal working day. Soon after the local minister arrived to tell Polly's mother that her husband and two other men had been drowned whilst cutting weeds on the River Stour. Six months earlier Polly's father, John Allen, had come home from the pub in tears. He refused to tell his wife what was wrong, but without giving any details said that he had seen something that meant he was not long for this world. He suffered from bouts of depression from that evening to the day he drowned.

Little other information is forthcoming on the phantom Lady in White of Blandford village. Is she the local vision of doom?

THE GHOST FROM THE SOUTH ATLANTIC
3 January 1840
Bratton Clovelly, Devon, England

The Rev. Sabine Baring-Gould's mother was quietly reading the Bible when she saw her brother Henry sitting near her but Henry was serving with the Navy in the South Atlantic at the time! Mrs Baring-Gould recognised the figure for what it was, an apparition at time of death, and calmly noted it in the Bible. A month later she heard that her brother had died near Ascension Island, on the date she had seen him.

THE DRUMMER OF CORTACHY
1844 and 1849
Cortachy Castle, Scotland

The origin of the ghostly drummer of Cortachy Castle dates back to the Middle Ages, when an ancestor of the Ogilvy's had a messenger from a despised chieftain pushed into a drum and thrown over the battlements. Before being killed the messenger vowed to haunt the family forever. Over several hundred years the family were plagued by ghostly drumming, which always seemed to anticipate a death in the family. During Christmas 1844 Miss Dalrymple, a guest at the castle, heard a drumming noise below her window as she was dressing for dinner. She mentioned it to her hosts Lord and Lady Airlie later, and was dismayed to see them turn pale and start whispering about the gloomy phophet of death. Miss Dalrymple heard the drumming again the following day, and cut short her visit.

Six months later Lady Airlie died, leaving behind a note saying that she knew the drumming was for her. The drumming was heard again on 19 August 1849 when a guest of the Ogilvys heard it as he was travelling across the moors to the castle. When he got there he heard that the 9th Earl of Airlie was seriously ill in London. He died the next day. The ghostly drummer has not been heard since though. Perhaps that's just as well.

THE GHOUL OF BERKELEY SQUARE
1870s and 1880s
50 Berkeley Square, London, England

Very much a Victorian sensation piece this one, and in its heyday it was dubbed 'The most haunted house in London', yet most of the story seems to belong in the realm of folklore. Number 50 was originally built for Prime Minister George Canning in the 18th century, but the haunting seems to stem largely from a later owner, a Mr Myers, who was rather an eccentric man much feared by the locals purely because he was so unusual. Mr Myers was said to have been jilted by his fiancée when he was a young man, and had never got over it, a story that would appeal to the morbidly romantic Victorians. In 1860 Myers bought the house and was said to live in a small room in the garrett, where he would only open the door to his manservant for food.

The neglected house fell into more and more disrepair, and took on a sinister appearance as its windows became encrusted with black dust and cobwebs. Curiously neighbours at this time reported the strange fact that the party walls adjoining the house were "saturated with electric horror". In 1873 Myers was summoned to court for tax evasion but he failed to appear and surprisingly the case was dropped. The local officials knew Myers was eccentric, and believed that was purely because he was living in a haunted house! By the time Myers died in the late 1870s the house had already a considerable reputation for being haunted, according to the local press. Numerous morbid stories began to circulate about past inhabitants dying insane because of things they had witnessed in the house.

On Christmas Eve 1887 two sailors arrived in London and went looking for cheap lodgings. They found 50 Berkeley Square boarded up and empty. It was ideal. They camped out in a top room, where they heard footsteps and saw an apparition of a shapeless thing. One escaped, but the other was found dead, impaled on the railings below the window. Locals also reported hearing strange noises from the house at this time, and of seeing books being hurled into the street. Since 1939 the house has been leased to Maggs Brothers, antiquarian booksellers. No ghostly phenomena has been reported. Nowadays 50 Berkely Square looks the epitome of clean respectability, and it is hard for us to see where the Victorians got their ideas.

THE DERRYGONNELLY POLTERGEIST
1877
Derrygonnelly, nr Enniskillen, Northern Ireland

Rapping noises frequently broke out at a house here. Psychic researcher Sir William Barrett attempted to communicate with the entity using a knocking technique. This was pretty pointless when it came to gathering information, for Sir William merely asked the poltergeist how many fingers were extended whilst his hand was in his pocket and the poltergeist guessed correctly each time.

THE OLD POST OFFICE HAUNTING
1892/1936
The Old Post Office, Royston, Hertfordshire, England

The sound of someone chopping wood plagued post office workers over a considerable period, resulting in many night-shift workers refusing to carry out their stints. One night the postmaster, John Freeman, heard the sound of smashing glass. The sound was confirmed by the night delivery man, but when they investigated in the morning no glass was found to be broken. Freeman also heard doors banging and footsteps, and on one occasion saw a key turning by itself in a lock. When the post office was turned into a community centre in 1936 the workmen renovating the building had almost exactly the same experiences as Mr Freeman.

THE ALLEGED HAUNTING OF BALLECHIN HOUSE

1897

Ballechin House, Perthshire, Scotland

This haunting was extensively investigated by Ada Goodrich-Freer, a member of the Society for Psychical Research, but not one of their most reliable investigators. There is plenty of evidence to suggest that Miss Goodrich-Freer was a compulsive liar and attention seeker. For example, a paper she wrote on second sight turned out to be a complete plagiarism of a piece written earlier by a Scottish priest. She was also caught cheating at a table-rapping session. On another occasion she investigated a haunted house in Surrey. She told the owners that the place wasn't haunted at all, but informed SPR members that she had seen a hooded female ghost there, although in all fairness, she might have been aware of the risk of libelling the reputation of a property, or simply anxious not to worry the owners of the home.

Her work on the alleged haunting of Ballechin House can still excite controversy even now. In 1897 Miss Goodrich-Freer heard that the house was said to be haunted by a former owner. This rather eccentric chracter wanted his corpse fed to his dogs when he died so that he could come back to life in their bodies, but naturally this disgusting request wasn't carried out, and the gentleman who had picked up strong ideas about reincarnation during many years spent in India, was said to be very annoyed about it. Miss Goodrich-Freer had rented it for a month, to all outward appearances for a fishing holiday. Once there she claimed to hear thumps, bangs and ghostly footsteps. She also said she had her bedclothes torn off her by a poltergeist, and witnessed a ghostly nun weeping in a nearby glen, after she had been instructed to go there at dusk during a ouija board session.

Guests who came to stay heard the thumps and footsteps, but didn't experience any of the more sensational aspects of the haunting. It was reported, rather tongue-in-cheek, that a hunchback had been seen walking upstairs, a priest heard saying his office and a phantom black squirrel, of all things, sighted. One male guest said he had seen a disembodied hand clutching a crucifix at the foot of his bed, and Miss Goodrich-Freer claimed to see two disembodied dog's paws on her bedside table. She returned to London to write *The Alleged Haunting of Ballechin House,* but was rather miffed to be surpassed in her endeavours by one of her guests, J Callendar Ross, who wrote a sarcastic piece about the haunting for *The Times*. An angry exchange of letters took place in the paper, which no doubt was greatly amusing for everyone else. The owner wasn't too happy either, at having his property exposed as a haunted house, especially a dubious one. Mr Callendar Ross wrote about "the suspicion and disgust that close contact with SPR tends to excite".

Naturally after this Miss Goodrich-Freer hitherto the pretty darling of a couple of the more elderly male members of the SPR, now found herself frozen out by them.

THE CORPUS CHRISTI COLLEGE HAUNTING

1904

Old Lodge, Corpus Christi College, Cambridge, England

A Master of the College, Dr Butts, was prone to depressions when he worked here in 1630. Then, on Easter Sunday 1632, he was found hanging in his room. His ghost began to be seen in the grounds soon after. Many years later, in 1904, a student living in the rooms opposite Butt's old ones, reported seeing an old man with long hair leaning out of the window and said he felt that the man was hostile. He ran across to the building, but found the doors locked, and learnt that everyone in the building had been out that afternoon. Six undergarduates attempted to hold an exorcism in the rooms during which they all felt an inexplicable chill, and a couple claimed to see a misty shape. When they tried holding out a crucifix to it, they said they were held back by an invisible wall of pressure.

Another group attempted an exorcism a few days later and had the same experience. The rooms were closed off at a later date.

THE BIRD OF DEATH

1917

Arundel Castle, Sussex, England

Ghost buster Eddie Burke said entering this castle was like "walking into a psychical mist" but it also has its very own prophet of doom, a phantom white bird that is said to flutter against the windows to warn of the impending death of a member of the family. For instance it appeared just before the death of the Duke of Norfolk in 1917.

THE BATTERSEA POLTERGEIST

November 1927

8 Eland Road, Battersea, London, England

The house was occupied by Henry Robinson, an 86-year-old invalid, his son Frederick, 27, his three daughters, and his 14 year-old grandson Peter. It began with objects raining down on the conservatory roof. When a policeman was called to the scene he was hit on the head with a lump of coal whilst standing in the back garden. On another occasion the Robinson's washerwoman found the wash-house full of smoke, and red hot cinders on the floor. She gave notice straight after. Ornaments were smashed, furniture over-turned and windows were broken. A chest of drawers in the old man's room turned over of its own accord and a journalist, Jane Cunningham, watched as lumps of coal, coins and washing-soda completely obliterated the conservatory roof.

Controversial ghost-hunter Harry Price investigated but witnessed little of any importance. Soon after Frederick had a nervous breakdown and had to be hospitalised. At the same time several chairs marched in single-file down the hallway. The old man was removed to hospital and one of the daughters fell ill, so the police advised them to leave the house for a while. A medium visited the empty house and began to shiver, but failed to identify a spirit. Frederick checked himself out of hospital and made arrangements for his family to live elsewhere. The haunting then ceased. But in 1941 Frederick confirmed Harry Price's sensational statement that slips of paper with writing on them had fluttered down out of nowhere.

One read "I am having a bad time here. I cannot rest. I was born during the reign of William the Conqueror". It was signed "Tom Blood". It seems unlikely that the house was haunted by someone from the Conq's day, but poltergeists are notorious liars at the best of times. Incidentally, just over the garden wall at the back of the house was a mental hospital for disturbed ex-servicemen. How much of their mental distress had the Robinson's unwittingly picked up? Most of the family suffered some kind of mental trauma over the poltergeist outbreak, but thankfully their troubles ceased when they left the house for good.

THE GHOST OF WILLIAM TERRISS
1928 (also 1956 and 1962)
Adelphi Theatre, London, England

One of the most famous ghosts of London's theatreland. William Terriss was a popular actor in his day, but a bit too popular for some tastes. On 16 December 1897 he was stabbed by a jealous bit-player, Richard Arbor Prince, who spent the rest of his life in a mental institution for the murder. According to legend, Terriss was supposed to have died in the arms of his leading lady and mistress Jessie Milward, uttering the fateful words "I'll be back". There were no reported sightings of Terriss until 1928 when a stranger in town, who knew nothing of the killing, saw a man in grey Victorian clothes in Maiden lane, just outside the theatre. He later saw a photograph of the man and recognised him as William Terriss.

At around the same time an actress, using Jessie Milward's old dressing-room, had her chaise-longue shaken, was gripped by an unseen force and saw a greenish light hovering above her mirror. Several years later, Terriss's ghost was seen by a variety of witnesses wafting around and inside the staff canteen of Covent Garden Underground Station. In 1962 night workmen saw the greenish light float across the stage of the theatre where it formed into the shape of a man. The apparition then parted the stage curtains and went into the stalls, tipping the seats as it progressed.

THE RETURN OF CAPTAIN HINCHCLIFFE

July 1928
Surrey, England

Captain WGR Hinchcliffe set out on 13 March 1928 with Elsie Mackay, to make the first east to west transatlantic flight. They never returned. They were believed to have crashed somewhere near the Azores. A few months later his wife Emilie heard footsteps pacing in her hallway. She visited a well-known medium Eileen Garrett, who informed her that it was her late husband, and that he had made the noises to comfort his wife with the idea that he was still around. If so, that makes him a unique ghost.

THE NICE LADY
1930s
Well Walk, Hampstead, London, England

The actor Leslie Banks lived with his family in a house here until his death in 1935. His three daughters frequently reported seeing the ghost of 'a nice lady in a violet silk dress' at the top of the stairs. She was never seen by the adults. After Banks's death the house was taken over by a couple called William and Patricia Johnson. One evening, as they were sitting in the living-room, Patricia noticed a wisp of smoke forming behind her husband's head. He wasn't smoking though. Over the next couple of years this phenomenon was sighted four or five times.

During WWII the house was taken over as a temporary home for poor people. They all reported experiencing strange incidents, such as objects moving, and coughing and groaning noises. Many blamed the haunting on the structural repairs that had to be carried out to transform it to its wartime usage. It is commonly believed that ghosts resent any kind of renovation work. During excavations a woman's skeleton was found beneath the kitchen floor.

THE MOST HAUNTED HOUSE IN ENGLAND
1930/39
Borley Rectory, Essex, England

The most amazing thing about the haunting of Borley Rectory is how it continues to fascinate, even after all these years. This is after the haunting has been torn to shreds, and practically everyone ever involved in the case has come out of it with their reputations sullied in one way or another. There seems little point in going over the history of a place that must surely be known by heart to anyone with even a passing interest in the supernatural. But here goes. It was built in 1863 by the Rev. Henry Dawson Ellis Bull for his enormous family. It was a gloomy Victorian monstrosity with dark rooms, ugly little turrets and harsh red brick. Local legend has it that it was built over the site of an old monastery, although there has never been a single shred of proof found for this.

The entire haunting seems to have been built around the apparition of a Grey Nun, sighted by many witnesses walking around the rectory garden. The Nun is one of the most dubious aspects of the case. Long after she has been discredited and revealed to be nothing more than bonfire smoke or a column of midges the sightings of the wretched woman have persisted. When Henry Bull died, his son Harry took over the rectorship. Harry was a strange man. It is highly possible that he was an alcoholic, for the rectory cellar was found littered with empty wine bottles after his death, and he also spent endless nights sitting up in the summerhouse wanting to catch a glimpse of the Nun.

He was emotionally volatile, taken to striking his stepdaughter because she didn't agree with his religious views, and bursting into tears if the car wouldn't start. Many have tried to claim that the haunting was going strong in Harry's time. It wasn't. The Nun was sighted occasionally, but as I have just said there is no substance for her existence at all. Harry was also driven to distraction by endless bouts of bell-ringing, when the service bells would ring all at once. But many years later a wire connected to the service bells was found hanging out of the ivy on the wall at the back of the house. Harry was considered a 'bit daft' in the village, and no doubt the locals enjoyed tormenting him with this practical joke.

After his death the rectory lay empty for some considerable time. This enhanced its spooky reputation no end, although its lack of amenities like electricity and running water may have influenced clergymen more than vague tales of ghostly apparitions. In 1929 the Rev. Guy Eric Smith and his wife Mabel moved in. The Smiths suspected the villagers of trying to drive them out. They had been without a proper rector for years, and didn't see the need for one now. Lights seen in disused rooms were thought later to be the reflections of passing trains, and footsteps heard in the house could have been due to the strange acoustics of the rectory. The house was built around the courtyard in a u-shape. The footsteps of anyone walking outside could have been amplified in the house.

At the time though, Mrs Smith believed the house was haunted, and Harry Price was called in. Borley Rectory was to both make and break Price. He spent over ten years involved in the case, but his investigation was torn to shreds by sceptics and other psychic investigators, and he was even accused, after his death, of faking the entire thing. To be fair to Price, I suspect there was a certain amount of' 'professional' jealousy going on. Price got two bestselling books out of the Borley haunting, and it made him a household name. This would have stuck in the throat of many others in the business. The Smiths moved out after a short while, and the Foysters moved in.

There must have been few families stranger than the Foysters. The Rev. Lionel Foyster, a cousin of Harry

Bull's, has always got off lightly in any assessment of his character, usually depicted as a saintly old man. In Robert Wood's sensational book *The Widow of Borley*, a different picture entirely is painted, showing Lionel to have been a voyeur, and even a possible paedophile. His wife Marianne was much younger than him. Lionel had baptised her when she was a little girl, and for that reason Lionel didn't think they should have conjugal rites. Instead a variety of strange men were brought to the rectory to satisfy Marianne's sexual needs. Marianne herself was given to dramatic gestures and fantasising.

Predictably the sceptics have had a field day with her involvement in the haunting. Soon after they moved in poltergeist phenomena, on a scale never seen before at the rectory, broke out. Objects flew through the air, bottles smashed, doors were locked and keys went missing. Marianne was punched by an unseen force, and fires broke out at random. *This is all very common poltergeist activity.* The rather eccentric set-up in the house would have provided a fertile background for the poltergeist activity at the house, as the details bear close resemblances to other such outbreaks all over the world. Sadly though it has been discredited because of the other ridiculous tales of phantom Grey Nuns, and the ghost of Harry Bull returning from beyond the grave with his will, which he wanted amending (this tale was said to have been perpetrated by his sisters, three spiteful old cats who were annoyed that Harry's widow was his sole beneficiary). At the core I believe the haunting was genuine, but it has grown so many layers that no one wants to take it seriously. Without all the romanticising that has gone on over Borley over several years, we would simply have just another poltergeist outbreak. The rectory burnt down on 27 February 1939. This had apparently been predicted in a seance a couple of years before, and that an entity calling itself 'Sunex Amurex' would be the one to ignite the flame. The actual details are much more prosaic. A few months before a Captain H Gregson bought the rectory, intending to make money out of its reputation. This idea lost its appeal rather quickly, and so he torched the place for its insurance money. Gregson lost his case.

Because the house was destroyed in such a spectacular fashion, the haunting has gone on over the years. The Grey Nun has been sighted running down the road, loitering in the churchyard, as well as on her beat in the garden. At times the Borley story has plumbed the depths of sensationalism. Even the burning of a chicken house in the village was tied in with the haunting. But, apart from being a genuine poltergeist outbreak, Borley must be credited with one thing. It has shown how the alleged haunting of a remote, gloomy rectory can maintain a firm grip on the public imagination for many years.

GRANDPA'S GHOST

February 1932
Wiltshire, England

Mrs Edwards and her daughter Mary watched one evening as Mrs Edward's father, Grandpa Bull, walked to her bedridden mother's side and place his hand on her forehead. Grandpa Bull had been dead for eight months. This was nothing unusual, the spectre of Grandpa Bull was often seen by most members of the family and appeared to be quite solid. The family was large and lived in squalor in a house that wasn't fit for human inhabitation. Sceptics believed the family's story as they thought they were only trying to get better accommodation, but when the family was interviewed by members of the Society for Psychical Research, they were believed to be genuine. And it is far from unusual for ghosts to manifest in squalid surroundings. After all most poltergeists thrive on such conditions.

THE ASH MANOR HAUNTING
1934/36
Ash Manor, Surrey

An anonymous family moved into the manor in June 1934. The previous owner had been extraordinarily willing to drop his price, so they instantly assumed something must be wrong with it. The new owner suspected the plumbing, but his wife thought it might be less prosaic than that. She felt extremely ill-at-ease in the old servants quarters, but this might have been brought on by the fact that the previous owner had told her the staff had all suddenly run away, (although it hadn't stopped him living there undisturbed for several years). Stamping noises then broke out in the attic and in November 1934 the owner was woken by violent hammering on his bedroom door. For several nights this always occurred at the same time, 3.35 AM.

Then one night he woke to find a little old man in his room. He wore a green smock and muddy breeches. His eyes were "malevolent and horrid" and he was dribbling at the mouth. The owner put his hands out but as they went through the figure, he fainted. When he came to, his wife went to hit the ghost but also put her fist straight through the phantom. The little man appeared more and more often, always at night. He would walk across their bedroom to a cupboard that used to be a priest's-hole. Eventually the family began to accept him, and the owner's wife found she could make him disappear just by trying to touch him. However, very unpleasant was the sight of his exposed windpipe, which suggested he had slit his throat.

Two psychic investigators said the house had been built on an old Druid's stone circle, and that the ghost was that of Henry Knowles, who had cut his throat open when a milkmaid rejected his advances in 1819. An amateur photographer succeeded in taking a picture of a dim shape on the landing in January 1936. Professional psychic investigator Nandor Fodor, was called to the scene in July. The family were concerned about what the haunting would do to their social reputation. Fodor slept in the haunted room himself but witnessed nothing. He did find though that the owner's daughter was prone to temper tantrums and was inordinately jealous of her mother, so he deduced that she could well be acting as the ghost's catalyst. American medium Eileen Garrett succeeded in coming up with another ghost entirely. This one was young with blond hair, and she said he had been tortured to death in a royal castle nearby (both Farnham and Guildford castles are in the area).

She went into a trance and revealed that, at around the time of the Battle of Agincourt, there had been a prison about 500 yards to the west of the house. The misery of the lost souls that had been imprisoned there had impinged greatly on the area. The ghostly man with the cut throat was thriving on their unhappiness to manifest himself, and also on that of the daughter of the house. Mrs Garrett's tortured man came through, and raged about an Earl of Buckingham who had offered him a considerable amount of money in exchange for his wife. He said his name was Charles Edward Henley, son of Lord Henley of Huntingdon.

After the medium's visit the ghost of the hideous old man continued to be seen. The psychical investigators returned to the house. This time Mrs Garrett had embarrassing news for the family. The ghost had accused them of using him to "get at" each other. The owner's wife broke down in tears and admitted to the sorry state they all lived in. She said her husband was a secret homosexual, she was on drugs and her daughter hated her because she was besotted with her father. The owner had also begun talking in his sleep, as though he was Charles Henley. Soon after the extraordinary confession by the owner's wife, the haunting ceased entirely.

The authenticity of Mrs Garrett's 'medieval phantom' is dubious though. No one could verify his existence, and the Olde English handwriting that he used to communicate with her, via Automatic Writing, was ridiculed by the experts. Fodor believed that that particular ghost was the product of Mrs Garrett's mind, but was in no doubt at all that the rest of the haunting had been genuine.

THE HAUNTING OF LITTLE GRATTON

1935

Little Gratton, nr Reigate, Surrey, England

Little Gratton was built by Sax Rohmer, the creator of the fiendish Fu Manchu character. Part of the panelling and other wood furnishings in the house came from the *Mauretania*, Rohmer's favourite ship. In bad weather he swore that the woodwork creaked as though it was the old ship itself moving. The house seemed to have the same sort of unlucky influence on people that phantom black hounds have. One maidservant remarked that the house had an atmosphere like a cemetery, and was later killed by a lorry outside the main gates. In the same lane two young boys had also been killed. A man had killed himself in a neighbouring house, and a gardener had hanged himself in the garden shed!

This very undesirable residence, (instead of being demolished as it should have been) was sold to speed ace Sir Malcolm Campbell, which is quite surprising for he was rumoured to be very superstitious, refusing to sit down to dinner if there were only 13 people at the table. Sir Malcolm related on how on one occasion all the windows in the house had blown out inexplicably. He also remarked, quite understandably, that he wished he had never bought the place.

THE ALDBOROUGH POLTERGEIST

November 1936
Aldborough Manor, North Yorkshire, England

This case was investigated by Nandor Fodor, Research Officer of the International Institute for Psychical Research. By the time he arrived the service-bells had rung non-stop for five days, doors opened and closed of their own accord, and two of the maids had seen an apparition above a cradle. Lady Lawson-Tancred, the owner, was worried that the haunting would eventually drive her out of her own home. But by the time Fodor arrived the haunting had already ceased, in the infuriating way that poltergeist outbreaks have of suddenly halting without any reason. One of the maids who had seen the apparition had suffered a nervous breakdown and left the manor.

The other maid had an almost mystical affinity with animals. She seemed to act as a magnet to them. Birds would willingly sit on her shoulders and Lady Lawson-Tancred believed the girl was acting as the poltergeist's catalyst and dismissed her. It seems to have worked, because as soon as she left the haunting ceased altogether.

THE GHOSTLY NUN
31 December 1939
Cheltenham, Gloucestershire, England

Margo Vincent Smith and the headmaster of the school here, both saw a nun sit down on the edge of the playground at 6.15 on the evening of New Year's Eve, even though there was no chair for her to sit on. When the headmaster tried to get closer to her, she disappeared. Exactly one year later Margo saw the nun again in exactly the same place. The headmaster meanwhile had stealthily crept along the edge of the playground and noted that the nun certainly appeared real enough. When he shone his torch at her she vanished, and the torch never worked again. The school is now a private house which, as is only too often the case, puts the kiss of death on any psychic investigation into the matter.

THE GHOSTLY BOOKWORM
1940s
nr Lincoln, Lincolnshire, England

John May was employed in the 1940s by a new owner to tidy up the garden of a house they had just bought. They wanted the work completed before moving in, so whilst he worked on the garden May lived in the empty house. There was no electricity connected, so he had to use candle -light and on his first night he toured the ground-floor at 10.30 to check that everything was secure before going upstairs to sleep on a camp-bed. Whilst checking the drawing-room though, the key fell out of the lock in the door and the sash window slammed shut. May was not a stranger to paranormal activity, so the event didn't worry him much.

On his second evening at the house, he was sitting reading a newspaper when the candle dimmed, and was then lifted up by an unseen force and dashed to the ground. When he went to bed that night he was disturbed by the pages of a book he had been reading, constantly turning over. May heard locally that the previous owner had been a reclusive old lady, who might be resenting the appearance of new faces on the scene. May performed an exorcism himself, and that seemed to quieten her.

THE HAMPTON COURT HAUNTING

WWII and 1966

Hampton Court Palace, London, England

Hampton Court has so many ghosts it practically deserves a book to itself. We have two interesting cases from the 20 century. During WWII a police constable saw an entire entourage of ghosts walking in the grounds, consisting of seven women and two men, whereas in 1966 a member of the audience at a professional light and sound performance, claimed to have seen Cardinal Wolsey standing beneath an archway. This rather suprised the producer of the play as Cardinal Wolsey wasn't featured in it.

THE HAUNTING OF GILL HOUSE

1940

Gill House, nr Broomfield, Cumbria, England

This old house, which in parts dates back to the 13th century, was used as a base for Land Army girls during WWII. From very early in their stay the girls heard noises coming from an old bedroom. Believing that rats were the cause, a vermin exterminator was called in, but the noises continued, until eventually footsteps could be heard. Those girls unfortunate enough to sleep there related terrifying tales of someone trying to choke them. The Women's Land Army sent two representatives, Miss Eouslby and Mrs Parkin, to talk to the warden of the house, Miss Mandale. The warden said that she herself hadn't experienced anything but she took the girls' stories very seriously.

Mrs Parkin tried to use tapping to communicate with the entity , and after making a few tentative knocks on a cupboard, a form appeared in the shape of a man, and made straight for her! Everyone felt a coldness accompanied by a horrid smell "like a leaking coffin". They all concluded that the room was haunted. Using a ouija board they attempted to make contact with the spirit. An entity calling itself 'Gerald Wreay' came though, claiming he had been a Jacobite during the reign of King George I. He warned them that he had dabbled in Black Magic during his lifetime, and evil spirits often came to the house. A clairvoyant confirmed later that the house was haunted by a man in tight fitting breeches and a girl, thought to be Wreay's maidservant.

To try and calm the Land Army girls, the representatives agreed to stay the night in the haunted room. They left before dawn in a disturbed state. The hostel was closed down very soon after. The present owner is reluctant to confirm the haunting, and resents any question of a psychic investigation.

THE ANNIVERSARY OF A MURDER
1942
Rushbrooke Hall, nr Bury St. Edmunds, Suffolk, England

In 1578 a woman was murdered here and thrown from a window into a moat. Since then it was rumoured that her murder was re-enacted every year at the same time. In 1942 ghost-hunter Peter Underwood, then at the start of his very long career, spent the night in the haunted room with three friends. At two o'clock in the morning the window slammed back against the wall and the group felt an icy blast. They then heard a distant 'plop' as though something had been dropped into the moat.

THE CONTENTED GHOST
1947
Perranporth, Cornwall, England

Two middle-aged ladies were annoyed to be allocated an old dilapidated chalet whilst they were on holiday, but nonetheless settled down to enjoy their break. At 11.30 PM they heard footsteps and a dog growling outside, but on looking out couldn't see anything amiss. After they had locked up for the night, they heard the chalet door open, then someone crossing the room and a sound as though pages of a newspaper were being turned. This was accompanied by a pleasant little chuckle. The women grabbed some objects as weapons and confronted their intruder. There was nobody there. All they could see was the motion of the rocking chair as though someone was sitting in it.

In spite of the ghost's contented nature, the women demanded to be moved the following morning. The site owner confirmed that many had complained about that particular chalet. The holiday complex is now demolished, and the identity of this refreshingly happy ghost will never be known.

THE BARNWELL CASTLE SEANCES
September/November 1948
Barnwell Castle, Northamptonshire, England

The ruined castle had been rumoured to be haunted for many years, and in September 1948 a local historian Tom Lichfield and a psychic friend undertook to hold a seance in the grounds. A former abbot of nearby Ramsey Abbey came on the psychic airwaves, to tell them that the castle had been used as a place of trial and execution in the 14th century (records confirmed this later). Another contact that came through was Marie LeMoyne, who claimed to have died whilst the castle was being built in 1266 and that her secret lay in a chest in the dungeon. She claimed to have been imprisoned there. Records confirmed that a Marie LeMoyne had died at the time the castle was built, and local folklore said that Berengarius LeMoyne had walled up a woman alive there.

Ten days later another seance was graced with the presence of the villain himself, who said he had had a lot on his mind at the time of the murder. In November a third seance was held in the north-east tower and Berengarius got in touch again. This time he announced he would 'fire' to warn them, and his words were immediately followed by a sharp crack and the sudden appearance of a ghostly monk. The terrified participants departed the castle rather quickly.

THE GHOST IN A HAT
1950
Southsea, Portsmouth, Hampshire, England

A young girl called Judy lived with her mother at her grandparent's house in Southsea after her father's death. The house was Edwardian and looked fairly ordinary, but both Judy and her mother felt there was something "very strange" about the building although her grandparents weren't bothered at all. On one occasion, though, her grandmother and her great-aunt were having tea alone in the house, when they saw a strange man leaning over the top of the stairs. The resolute old ladies each grabbed a poker and set off in pursuit of the intruder. There was no one there. On another occasion Judy saw what appeared to be the shape of "a man in a Homburg hat" standing just outside her grandfather's room.

Judy also felt a presence in her room at night. She would hear somebody crossing the floor and then creaks as they sat down in a wicker chair. Her family were concerned and moved her to another room. But this was even worse. Judy would wake at night certain that something awful was standing in the corner of the room. She said it seemed to "pulsate", and she lay rigid in bed with terror. Her grandparents tried to convince her that it was just childish nightmares, but Judy remained certain that it wasn't. After her grandparents' deaths many years later Judy's mother went to the house to clear out their things. She remarked that although it was summer, and the house had been sealed for two weeks, it was dreadfully cold.

THE OLD MAN IN HIS NIGHTGOWN
1950
Anglesey, Wales

A house here, lived in by a couple called Peter and Bridget and their three-year-old son Oliver, was visited by self-styled 'holy ghostbuster' the Rev. J Aelwyn Roberts. The cause for concern was that every night without fail Oliver would come downstairs at precisely nine o'clock, as though he was sleepwalking. When questioned Oliver said that an old man in a long nightgown and a 'Noddy' cap would come into his room and "shoo" him out of bed. A psychic friend of the Rev. Roberts, Elwyn Roberts, said that the ghost liked to pace around the room but Oliver's bed was in the way. He suggested that they move the bed. Peter and Bridget obliged, and Oliver was no longer pestered by the old man.

An elderly neighbour told them that a retired navy man, a Captain Lucas, used to live in the house. Towards the end of his life he had become addicted to whisky, and would roam the house in his night-clothes, never bothering to get dressed.

THE COLLEGE HAUNTING
1950
Oxford University, Oxford, England

Peter Edwards was rather disappointed to find when he moved into his student accommodation that it was so quiet, especially considering he was sharing the building with about 300 other students. Nevertheless, in the middle of the night Peter was woken by excited shouting coming from the quadrangle beneath his window. He heard footsteps pounding up the stairs, assaults on a door and somebody yelling for something to be "cut down". Irritated that he might be the victim of a practical joke, Peter went to confront his tormentors. But when he flung open his door the corridor was completely empty and silent ... as silent as the grave.

Peter spilled his whole story to one of the dons the following morning. The don told him that there had been two suicides in Room 16, one during the 1850s and one in 1908. Peter could have unwittingly eavesdropped on an action replay of either unfortunate event.

THE FRUSTRATED MOTHER
1952
Tunbridge Wells, Kent, England

One night Mr Robert Hughes woke up to find a woman leaning across him and staring intently at his young son Malcolm, sleeping next to him in bed. He said she appeared to be in her mid-40s, wore her hair in a bun, and was wearing a heavy dull-coloured dress. As he watched she glided away and slowly vanished. According to his wife the previous owner had been a Mrs Ada Phillips, who had desperately wanted children. She and her husband arranged to adopt a baby, but the night before the child was due to arrive at the house Mrs Phillips tragically died. Mr Hughes saw the woman four times over the next 20 years. On one occasion he went to grab her but she was insubstantial, like "cigarette smoke".

THE ARDACHIE LODGE HAUNTING
1952
Ardachie Lodge, Loch Ness, Highlands, Scotland

Peter McEwan and his wife moved here to breed pigs, and they hired a Mr and Mrs McDonald to look after the house. On the first night the McDonalds heard footsteps outside the room, although there was no-one there. Mrs McDonald saw an old woman beckoning towards her. The couple moved to another room, but this time Mrs McDonald saw an old woman crawling along the corridor! The previous owner had been a Mrs Brewin, a rather eccentric old lady, who for reasons best known to herself, had liked crawling around her house late at night. The McEwans and the McDonalds left the house very soon after, and the building was pulled down.

Psychic researcher Stephen Jenkins discovered that the house had stood on a node where four ley lines crossed so it is suppossed that the ghost of Mrs Brewin may well have been drawing her psychic energy from these lines.

THE RUNCORN POLTERGEIST
1952
1 Byron Street, Runcorn, Cheshire, England

A rather crowded household this, so much so that 16 year old John Glynn had to share a double bed with his grandfather, Samuel Jones. The hauntings started when rappings broke out on the dressing-table in their room, followed by drawers moving. During a seance held by the medium, Philip France, two Bibles were flung around the room. A couple of weeks later a clock was thrown across the bedroom and was witnessed by a reporter from the *Runcorn Guardian*. He also thought he heard the dressing-table being moved, but nothing was out of place. More reporters were called to the scene and witnessed the dressing-table moving, a chair thrown against the wall, a clock crashing to the floor and a carpet was moved from one side of the room to another.

One reporter was hit on the head by four books. A neighbour, Mrs E Dowd, didn't believe the entity would chuck anything at her and was promptly hit in the face with a heavy book. Bedclothes and pillows were also moved around. The activity ceased at six in the morning. Several priests were called to the house, and one, the Rev. Stevens, was also hit with a book, and saw a heavy box turn over. The Rev. asked the poltergeist to knock three times in response. John Glynn was sitting on a chair in the middle of the room and restrained by the priests, but the dressing-table and a blanket chest still continued to move.

John Glynn was put to bed, and the Rev. Stevens witnessed a jigsaw, that had been on the dressing-table, fly across the room. Police officers on another occasion saw furniture moving and books flying through the air. Attempts to photograph the phenomena failed as the poltergeist seemed shy of cameras and would refuse to perform. As if all this wasn't enough a minor war broke out between the other local newspapers, jealous at the monopoly the *Runcorn Guardian* had on the case. *The Runcorn Weekly News* accused Samuel Jones of committing fraud and although Jones invited them to his house, no poltergeist antics were forthcoming.

The entire phenomena ceased after three eventful months. During this time Jones had been working part-time on a local farm. Throughout the haunting all the 53 pigs in his care inexplicably died. The farmer and his wife also saw a mysterious black cloud floating around the farmyard, and drawers moved inside the house. The farmer visited the house in Byron Street and saw the black cloud hanging over Jones's bed. During this visit he also had his coat thrown over his head several times. The farmer's wife once saw Jones leaving the farm and the black cloud following him. Whatever was the cause behind the case, I feel it is certain that the haunting was activated by the chronic overcrowding in the house in Byron Street.

THE WHITECHAPEL POLTERGEIST
1952
88 Newark Street, Whitechapel, London, England

Harry Conway's seven year old son was terrified by icy fingers that would grab at his bedclothes at night. It became so frightening that the little boy became a nervous wreck, and the family decided to move. The family had also experienced trouble when their son's bedroom door was found locked for no reason, and an aunt who came to stay also felt the sensation of someone pulling at her bedclothes. In June 1954 Harry and Brenda Cox moved into the property, to set up a small sewing business and another couple called Alec and Vera Bessell, employed by the Coxs', moved into the ground floor. Very soon footsteps were heard coming from the top floor.

The Coxs' also heard footsteps outside their bedroom door, but no one was there. One evening, whilst the

Coxs' were out, the Bessells heard sweeping noises coming from their room. In the early hours of one morning the Coxs' felt their bedclothes being pulled away from them. Harry Cox admitted that this caused his hair to literally stand on end! One evening they all heard heavy, measured footsteps walking down the front stairs but no one was there. Doors that should have been locked were found unlocked, and vice versa. A guest, Michael Winter, arrived to stay, and slept in the living-room. He woke up in the night to see a number of coat-hangers which had been on rails, flying around the room. Brenda and Vera noticed jugs and tumblers moving in the kitchen. When Harry Cox's parents visited, the old man heard a sound "like a cat in pain" coming from a glass-fronted cabinet but there was nothing there to explain it. A medium said the haunting was being caused by the ghost of an old man with a wooden leg. In time the poltergeist activity faded away. The building is now derelict.

THE GHOSTLY KILTED HIGHLANDERS

November 1956

Cuillin Hills, Isle of Skye, Scotland

Geology student Peter Zinovieff and his half-brother Patrick Skipworth were camping out in this area when they witnessed, at three o'clock one morning, a montage of kilted Highlanders storming across the stony ground. The following night they had the same experience, but one hour later, at 4.00 AM.

Mr Ian Campbell, owner of the nearby Sligachan Hotel said he believes the ghostly soldiers to have been Jacobite rebels from 1745.

THE GHOST FROM THE PICTURE
31 December 1956
Stainland, nr Halifax, Yorkshire, England

Mr Paradise, who had lived in his cottage since he was a small boy in 1920, was lying in bed on this particular New Year's Eve listening to music on his radio. Suddenly he became aware that a face was forming in the picture over the mantelpiece, and then, even more incredibly, a figure seemed to step out of the picture and head towards him. Mr Paradise described the figure as having a white face and long flowing hair. Not only that, but the figure was sawing away on a violin! Mr Paradise did not appreciate this impromptu entertainment and fled the room in terror.

A few nights later he was standing in the kitchen when he felt a presence of someone standing behind him. He admitted to being too afraid to turn around. Soon afterwards the bedroom fireplace was bricked up, and that seems to have put an end to any more escapades from the ghost with the violin.

THE GHOST OF DOUGLAS JARDINE
19 June 1958
Lord's Cricket Ground, London, England

Colonel D Pritchard was sitting in the pavilion bar when he saw Douglas Jardine sitting a few feet away. (Jardine was the cricket captain notorious for his controversial 'Bodyline' technique). The Colonel raised his glass at Jardine and the captain raised his in return. A few minutes later Pritchard went over to have a few words with his old friend, but he couldn't find him. It was later announced on the loudspeaker that Jardine had died in Switzerland the day before.

THE CHATHAM HAUNTING
1960s
Magpie Hall Road, Chatham, Kent, England

Two neighbouring houses were plagued for many years by the sounds of rappings and footsteps when the lights were put out. The noises would begin at midnight and end about five in the morning, and always stopped when a light was switched on. A man was said to have slit his throat in one of the houses a few years before. A vaguely-described "form" was also seen by one of the occupants.

THE SUICIDAL FARMER
1960s
Llangefni, Anglesey, Wales

Farmer Brian James was found shot dead at his home near Llangefni. At the inquest suicide was ruled out, even though he had been beset with problems prior to his death, and it was agreed that his rifle had gone off accidentally whilst he was climbing over a stile. Brian had whistled through his teeth whenever he was worried, and five months after the funeral, his wife Bethan, heard the same noise in the house. Bethan realised it was Brian's ghost, and found the experience too traumatic to live with, so she moved to a cottage in a nearby village. The whistling noise followed her there. Bethan called in the local 'holy ghostbuster' the Rev. Aelwyn Roberts.

He went to Bethan's house with his friend, a research scientist called Elwyn Roberts. Both confirmed that Brian was standing in the hallway. Brian communicated to Bethan that he had committed suicide, but he regretted it. He felt he had to explain to Bethan, and apologise to her. He had tried shouting "sorry" to her, but she hadn't heard him. After this 'beyond the grave confession' the haunting ceased.

THE NEWBY HOODED SPECTRE

Early 1960s

Newby, nr Ripon, Yorkshire, England

A very eerie-looking ghost was photographed at the church here. It appeared on a photograph of the altar taken by the Rev. K F Lord. The mysterious spectre stands in hooded, voluminous robes by the altar rail with a mask over its face, looking like the sort of ghost one wouldn't like to meet on a dark night!

THE CURSE OF THE PAINTING

1960

Clarendon Drive, Putney, London, England

Mrs Dorothy Jenkins bought a painting in a junk shop. It showed a woman in a red velvet dress and was signed simply 'Antoine'. Mrs Jenkins was beset with problems after her purchase but was strangely advised not to sell it as her problems would only increase and both she and her son suffered nervous breakdowns soon after the purchase of the painting. A well known medium, Ena Twigg, was called in but did not come alone for by now Leslie Howard (the assistant editor of the *Psychic News* and Ena's husband), three newspaper reporters and a photographer were all showing an interest in the case. Mrs Twigg recoiled in horror on seeing the painting.

She spoke of seeing blood, a confined space and electric shock therapy. All this related little to the painting itself more to the treatment Mrs Jenkins's son was enduring at that time. She also saw a bright light darting about the room. Little came of all this, as Mrs Twigg seems to have taken offence at the sceptical attitude of the newspapermen, and so the 'Curse of the Painting' and its depressive influence remains infuriatingly unsolved.

THE OTTERBURN ARMY
November 1960
Otterburn, Northumberland, England

Otterburn is where the Scots defeated the English in 1388. Centuries later Mrs Dorothy Strong saw a re-enactment of the battle from a taxi. She reported how the fare-meter in the taxi went haywire at the same time and the engine died. The spectral soldiers got closer then faded altogether.

THE GHOST OF HERNE THE HUNTER
1962
Windsor Great Park, Berkshire, England

The ghost of Herne the Hunter, the royal huntsman of King Richard II, is said to appear here, complete with a baying pack of phantom black hounds, at times of national crisis. In 1962 a group of young lads found a horn in a clearing in the forest. They blew on it for a joke and were quite astonished to hear another horn answering their call, as well as the barking of hounds. Suddenly Herne and his dogs came thundering towards them. The boys dropped the horn and fled.

THE DURHAM POLTERGEIST
1963/64
Bronte Street, Durham, England

The Coulthard family's council house was the scene of a poltergeist outbreak. During it objects were thrown, bottles and crockery were smashed, slippers flew into the air, and chairs were moved. A vicar was called in to perform an exorcism but it had no effect, and the family eventually had to leave their undesirable residence.

THE STOW-ON-THE-WOLD POLTERGEIST
1963/64
Chapen Street, Stow-on-the-Wold, Gloucestershire, England

A spirit nicknamed 'George' (typical nickname for ghosts) haunted a semi-detached house here. 'George' started out violently but reformed into a jolly old soul, frequently singing and joking. 'George's' first trick had been to cause the formation of pools of water in several rooms. Three plumbers, the head of the water board and a sanitary inspector failed to discover the cause of this tiresome event. Tapping broke out, furniture moved, the son of the house, David Pethrick, 14, was tipped out of bed, sheets were torn, a dressing-gown was rammed under the mattress, scratching noises were heard from David's bed, and the headboard was scarred.

Writing appeared on the walls, wallpaper was ripped off in parts and Mrs Nancy Pethrick saw a hand appear at the end of her son's bed, which started out as the size of a baby's and grew to that of a man's. David was very much the epicentre of 'George's' activities, and his voice was always heard in David's vicinity. 'George' claimed to be one of the builders of the house, and had died 20 years before on 15 February. The haunting had commenced on that date. When the family went on holiday 'George' went with them, and during a visit to a church he caused the walls to reverberate with tapping noises. Like a lot of poltergeist outbreaks this one has sparked controversy, and there is much to suggest that like Topsy in *Uncle Tom's Cabin* this story just grew and grew.

THE FARINGDON POLTERGEIST
1963/64
Oriel Cottage, Wicklesham Road, Faringdon, Oxfordshire, England

Oriel Cottage was inhabited by Mr and Mrs Wheeler, their son, 19, and their three daughters, aged 15, 10 and five. During the course of the haunting there were inexplicable bangings, rumblings, wafts of cold air and 'strange shadows' were sighted. On one occasion 21 people camped out in the cottage to catch a glimpse of the ghost, and all reported feeling a cold draught around their feet and seeing a 'mysterious shape'. For a fortnight at the height of the haunting, the girls would refuse to sleep upstairs and would spend the night huddled around the fireplace instead. What was especially annoying was that the Wheelers had lived in the cottage for 18 years undisturbed, prior to the poltergeist outbreak.

When Mrs Wheeler came close to having a nervous breakdown because of the events, her husband ripped up the floorboards to try and find a solution to it all, and architects were called in to check for flaws in the structure, but no conclusion was reached. In the end a medium was called in who said that the haunting was being caused by a former inhabitant of the cottage, who had committed suicide there. An exorcism was performed by Canon Christopher Harman and that seemed to lay the ghost, although why it took 18 years to make its presence felt is a mystery, unless one takes into consideration that one of the children in the house was being used as its catalyst.

THE CHEETHAM HAUNTING
1964
Cheetham, Greater Manchester, England

The sound of a child crying and a mournful whistling noise were heard at a house here. A dressing table was also moved across a room, a pram shook whilst the baby slept inside it and the apparition of an old woman was sighted. The family had a session with a planchette which revealed that a baby had once been murdered in the house. It instructed them to look inside the chimney. They did so and found a strip of calico sheeting, newspapers dating back to 1922 and a pencilled music score of the tune that they could hear being whistled. Later some small bones were unearthed from underneath the kitchen floor.

The family were fairly disappointed to be told these were of a cat or rabbit, not the murdered baby. The moral of this story is, *never trust a planchette. They are not reliable and can cause a great deal of unnecessary distress.*

THE BOSCOMBE HAUNTING
1964
Boscombe, Hampshire, England

The ghost in the flat belonging to Margaret Best, 28, liked to tuck her into bed at night! For nine months Margaret would wake up in the middle of the night to feel someone fussing around her divan tucking in the bedclothes. Objects in her bedroom would also be found moved. Less pleasant was the sensation she experienced of being strangled, after which marks would appear on her throat. After a short time the entire haunting then ceased, never to start again.

THE ROEBUCK HOTEL HAUNTING

mid-1960s

The Roebuck Hotel, Reading, Berkshire, England

Mysterious footsteps paced the corridors of this basic unembellished hotel late at night for several years. Locked doors and windows were also known to open of their own accord, furniture was moved and a loud hammering broke out on the doors. In February 1966 the them landlord, Alex Wolfenden, reported that the centre of the haunting seemed to be in the Admiral's Room and for that reason he wouldn't let anyone sleep there. The room is named after an Admiral who supposedly died in mysterious circumstances in the old house over 200 years ago. Rumours are that he burnt to death, although no clue to this mysterious admiral's identity has ever been uncovered. At one time four rooms in the oldest part of the hotel were left unused because the landlord thought guests might be too frightened by the things that went on there. All very sensational, but nothing supernatural has happened here for years now.

THE PHANTOM HITCH-HIKER OF HALSALL MOSS
1965
Halsall Moss, nr Ormskirk, Lancashire, England

At 11.30 PM on a Friday night at the beginning of the year a 24 year-old man was driving across Halsall Moss, an isolated peaty area, when he had a considerable shock. On glancing in his rear mirror he saw that an old gentleman wearing a flat cap and a white cravat was sitting on the back seat of his car! The driver stopped and nervously looked around, but the old man had disappeared. A few years later at a cocktail party the driver met another man who also claimed to have had exactly the same ghostly experience on Halsall Moss. Both agreed that there was nothing remotely threatening about the phantom hitch-hiker.

THE GREY LADY OF NETLEY
1966
Victoria Military Hospital, Netley, Southampton, Hampshire, England

When the hospital was demolished in 1966 the apparition of a woman in a Victorian nursing costume was sighted walking down the passage that led to the chapel. This apparition, known as the Grey Lady, had haunted the building for many years and was believed to be the ghost of a nurse of the Crimean War who, if local legend is to be believed, threw herself from an upstairs window after accidentally administering a fatal drug to a patient.

She was often sighted by night duty staff, and some fanciful theorists like to believe that she is the ghost of Florence Nightingale, who had ordered the building of the hospital. The 1966 sighting of her was held by some to be a protest on her part at the demolition of the hospital. Of course it was.

THE DUNSTABLE MAN IN BLACK

Summer 1966

Dunstable, Bedfordshire, England

Valerie Haywood, 19, often noticed an old man in black Victorian clothes loitering in one of the bedrooms at her home. He generally appeared in the early evening and had a disturbing effect on the family dog which refused to go into the room. They heard rumours that a man had gone insane in one of the bedrooms many years before.

THE PONTEFRACT POLTERGEIST

1 September 1966/1969

East Drive, Pontefract, Yorkshire, England

One of those numerous council house poltergeist outbreaks now, but this one is a real aristocrat. Water would appear inexplicably on the floor, objects were moved, and there was even a sighting of a hooded spectre. The Pritchard family nicknamed the ghost 'Fred' and 'Mr Nobody'. 'Fred' clocked up an astonishing list of poltergeist phenomena which puts the

Enfield and Borley Rectory hauntings to shame. Aside from the phenomena already mentioned loud breathing noises were heard, as well as drumming and banging. Mr and Mrs Pritchard's teenage daughter Diane was dragged upstairs, with marks left on her throat as a result.

Footprints were found inside the house. House keys flew down the chimney. A white mohair coat was found hidden in a pile of coal, but when retrieved the coat was completely clean (this haunting does sound suspiciously like another Topsy tale in parts). Inverted crosses were drawn on a wall. Jam was smeared on the doors and stairs. One sceptical witness, Aunt Maude, had a jug of milk poured over her head by the entity. The entity also enacted a bizarre game with Aunt Maude's fur gloves, which were said to jig when she sang *Onward Christian Soldiers*! The plug was taken from the tape-recorder when efforts were made to record the noises made by the ghost.

A grandmother clock was thrown down the stairs, and bedclothes were torn from the bed whilst the occupant was still in it. The smell of heavy perfume was detected. Especially disturbing was the occasion when a photograph of the Pritchards was found slashed. The hooded spectre seen in the house was thought to be a monk, hanged for rape during Tudor times. At the time of Henry VIII a gallows was reckoned to stand near where the house stands now. The activity ended when the family hung cloves of garlic around the house. Colin Wilson, a prolific writer on the paranormal, investigated and concluded that Philip, the 15 year old son, was the poltergeist's catalyst.

The house became something of a tourist attraction in the area, and bus-drivers would point it out to passengers and even stop to let them get a good look.

People who sat outside the house on vigil at night noted a strange glow around it! It must have seemed very dull in Pontefract after the haunting came to an end in 1969.

THE WEST HARTLEPOOL HAUNTING
1967
18 Dorset Street, West Hartlepool, Cleveland England

Mr and Mrs Parker, and their two year old daughter, fled from their house and went to stay with their next door neighbours, because having experienced some weird phenomena in the house, they were afraid to stay there. Two seances were held afterwards. In one, a man's head was seen outlined on the window curtains, and in another, a figure was seen standing in front of the fireplace. It was recognised as that of a deceased relative.

THE HORDEN HAUNTING
1967
4 Eden Street, Horden, Durham, England

A miner and his wife were disturbed by inexplicable events at their house and, although extremely reluctant to talk about what happened, they called in the local vicar, the Rev. T Matthews to perform an exorcism. The vicar's prayers failed to halt the events and the couple moved out, still reluctant to describe exactly what had gone on, except to say that "ghostly presences" had made themselves felt.

THE HAUNTED PHOTOGRAPHER'S STUDIO

1967

Ealing, London, England

A film was made about this haunting in which many of the witnesses spoke of their experiences. The phenomena included lamps swinging in unison, footsteps and voices heard, and people were touched by an invisible presence. A seance was held in which it was revealed that the house next door to the studio had been the site of a murder in 1943, when an airman had killed a woman and a child. He was hanged for the crime. During the seance the airman protested his innocence. Mysterious marks also appeared on the photographer's neck and arm.

THE EMNETH HAUNTING

1967

Emneth, Norfolk, England

An isolated old cottage played host to a restless haunting during the 1960s. The inhabitants, a couple by the name of Thorpe, reported that windows opened of their own accord, door latches moved, ornaments and furniture were broken, and the radio, television, cooker and alarm clock were all activated at different times when no one else was in the room. Mr Thorpe said that it often felt as though someone was in the spare bedroom. Eerie.

THE SIGHTING OF HARRY EVANS

January 1967
Dulwich, London, England

Mrs Cynthia Aspinall saw her old friend Harry Evans, whom she hadn't met for some time, standing in the garden of his house. Mrs Aspinall was concerned that Harry, who was 75, should be out in cold weather without a coat on, but when she spoke to him he looked right through her without saying a word. Mrs Aspinall was shocked to be told by Harry's sister, Kitty, that he had died a month before. Enquiries revealed that Harry had died of leukaemia at Dulwich Hospital in mid-December 1966.

GREAT AUNT'S NIGHTGOWN

January 1967
Leicester, England

Mrs Jennie Morrison's great aunt had left a last wish that she was to be buried in her favourite nightgown, but Mrs Morrison's mother had decided that it was too good to be hidden in a coffin and the nightdress was given to Jennie. The first time Jennie wore it though she woke up in the night to find her sleeve being pulled so violently that the was nearly dragged out of bed. Jennie took off the nightdress and threw it out onto the landing, where she heard a deep sigh, like that of an old woman. Predictably, she never wore the nightdress again.

THE GHOSTLY MONK OF CAISTOR

January 1967

Caistor, Lincolnshire, England

The church at Caistor has long been rumoured to be haunted by a ghostly monk playing the organ. The Vicar, Canon Ernest Pitman, left a tape-recorder running in the locked church overnight. When it was played back the sounds of footsteps, organ music and loud banging noises had all been picked up in the empty church.

THE HAUNTED PRISON

January 1967

Shepton Mallet, Somerset, England

The old prison at Shepton Mallet is said to be haunted by a White Lady, the ghost of a woman who was beheaded there in 1680. At this time there were also reports of an unnerving haunting that centred on the night duty room. The sound of heavy breathing was heard, plus a vague feeling of someone invisible in one room, inexplicable bangings, and the atmosphere in the room was decidedly unpleasant. The prison governor spent a night in the room himself and sent a report to the Home Office, in which he said that he could find no satisfactory explanation for the events. Two priests were called in to give a pep talk to the staff, and irritated them by telling them to try and forget about the eerie occurrences but this is easier said than done.

One officer reported that he often felt an icy feeling on the back of his neck, and also the sensation of being pushed when he was locking the door, even though he was alone, as he was on the one occasion when he felt as though somebody was trying to pin him down by the neck. From then on he refused to do another stint in the infamous night duty room. In recent years all is reported to be well again though.

THE GHOST AT THE GRAVESIDE

August 1967

Dartmoor, Devon, England

Fresh flowers have appeared inexplicably on a roadside grave two miles north of Widecombe-in-the-Moor for several years now. In the early years of the 19th century a girl called Mary Jay hanged herself in a barn which used to stand by the road. According to the custom of the time a suicide couldn't be buried in consecrated ground, so Mary Jay was laid to rest beside the road. The origin of the flowers may or may not have a supernatural explanation (it could just be one of many Dartmoor legends) but in 1967 a 17-year-old girl and her boyfriend saw a man, wearing a robe that looked like an old blanket, huddled by the grave. The blanket was also draped over his head and he appeared to have no face. Who or what the man was remains unknown, but the flowers keep on coming. Mary Jay though may have some links with the haunted 'Olde Inn' at nearby Widecombe. Some people believe she might have been a servant girl there.

THE GHOST ON THE SECURITY MONITOR

September 1967
Grimsby, Humberside, England

The haunting of a council house here was probably the very first occasion that a ghost has been recorded on a security monitor! Mr Ted Barning had the apparatus fitted after he and his family had been plagued by the entity for several weeks. The equipment was put in one of the bedrooms where most of the phenomena had taken place, and the monitor screen was watched downstairs by six members of the family and the electrical engineer who had fitted the equipment. All saw the face of an 'old man of hideous appearance' appear on the screen. One of the witnesses rushed upstairs and the face disappeared.

The engineer tested the equipment for faults but concluded that there was no explanation for the old man's sudden appearance on camera. The Barnings moved out soon after.

THE RETURN OF KEVIN FIRMIN

December 1968
Yorkshire, England

Kevin Firmin died of throat cancer at 3 o'clock in the afternoon of Christmas Eve 1955. For 13 years his widow Mary spent Christmas at home as a kind of homage to her late husband. But in 1968 she decided to spend it with her sister Joan instead. One afternoon, just before Christmas, she was walking to the village shops with her sister when she felt a peculiar buzzing in her ears, and looking towards the graveyard where Kevin was buried, she saw her husband gesturing to someone standing next to him. It was Joan's bachelor son Gordon, whom she had seen only that morning, alive and well. Mary felt that she couldn't tell Joan what she had seen, although she was visibly disturbed.

On Christmas Eve Gordon went to the local pub for a drink, and the women were to join him there later, and as they arrived at the pub they saw Gordon's van outside. Inside though was a considerable commotion for Gordon had suddenly collapsed and died. Mary believed she had seen a premonition of his death.

THE PALACE HOTEL HAUNTING
1969
Palace Hotel, Southport, Lancashire, England

The hotel was in the process of being demolished in 1969 when the demolition team reported some inexplicable incidents in the building. Voices were heard from the empty rooms and corridors on the second floor, and although the electricity had been cut off many weeks before, the lift moved up and down of its own accord. On one occasion nine of the workers entered the foyer and witnessed all the doors slamming at once, and the lift shooting up to the second floor. The winding room was investigated, and the brake for the lift was found firmly in the 'on' position. The emergency winding handle for cranking the lift had been removed prior to the demolition.

It was decided to cut the wires to the lift, but the blessed thing now refused to budge and wouldn't do so until it had been thumped with 28 pound hammers for nearly half-an-hour. During a T.V. broadcast a dog refused to pass the second floor landing, although he was perfectly alright in the rest of the building. The whole mystery remains completely unsolved.

THE GHOST OF MARY BLANDY
1969
Kenton Theatre, Henley-on-Thames, Oxfordshire, England

In 1752 Mary Blandy, a girl who lived in Henley-on-Thames, was hanged at Oxford for poisoning her father. In 1969 a play about Mary, *The Hanging Wood* by Joan Morgan, was produced at the Kenton Theatre, and many believe Mary's ghost disrupted the entire proceedings. During rehearsals a large mirror " jumped off" the wall, lights were switched on and off, doors opened and closed, and a young girl was sighted standing at the back of the theatre watching the performance, although no one saw her enter or leave the theatre. On one occasion members of the cast were discussing Mary when a cup jumped off the table and smashed on the floor.

The playwright said that she had sighted the girl's apparition herself many years before, when the trial of Mary Blandy was re-enacted at Henley Town Hall. She had also been seen by other witnesses.

THE PHANTOM ARMY

4 January 1969

Hare and Hounds Inn area, nr Havenstreet, Isle of Wight, England

A spectacular military montage was sighted in this area when Dr and Mrs White, whilst out driving at night, saw Saxon-type phantom soldiers in a phantom landscape. As they approached the *Hare and Hounds Inn,* which is bang in the centre of the island, they could see the whole building bathed in light and figures carrying flame torches running across the road. Some 20 yards from the inn, the entire mirage vanished, leaving only the inn in its more customary condition.

THE NEW MOSTON POLTERGEIST

May 1969

New Moston, Greater Manchester, England

A poltergeist invaded a council house here. The building was continuously bombarded with bricks, stones and milk bottles. Police were put on watch to await the culprit, but suspiciously on those nights the bombardments did not occur.

THE LANDLORD'S WIFE
June 1969
Wales

Detective Inspector D Elvet Price, of the Metropolitan Police, was spending the night at a Welsh inn. As he was going to the bathroom he saw a woman in a long old-fashioned dress walking towards him. He greeted her but she walked past without saying a word. Twice in the night he awoke to hear gasping and choking sounds in his room. He also felt an intense coldness. When it happened a third time he left his light on which seemed to stop the noises. He later found out that a former landlady at the inn, Angharad Llewelyn, had been beaten and strangled in an upstairs room on 30 August 1920. It transpired that on the evening of her death she had argued with her husband, a man with a volatile temper, and had gone upstairs and refused to come down.

A lodger, Dai Richards, said that he had tried to help Angharad but had fallen asleep before he could do so. He claimed that the landlord had drugged his beer. The judge believed Llewelyn had not intended to kill his wife and gave him a five year sentence. Price checked that the woman he had seen wasn't simply another guest and learnt that he was the only guest at the inn that night.

THE URINE GHOST
1970s
Warrington, Cheshire, England

A school that had been turned into a shop was, according to the shop staff, haunted. Puddles of a liquid that looked suspiciously like urine would appear on the floors. There was no cat on the premises and the building was kept locked at night. One customer, a religious woman, told the staff that she would pray for the disgusting phenomenon to stop. Unfortunately, the liquid then started appearing on her bedclothes at home! The staff believed the phenomenon at the shop was being caused by the ghosts of schoolchildren.

THE GHOSTLY CHORISTER
1970s
Marton, Gainsborough, Lincolnshire, England

The church in the small hamlet of Marton is reputedly haunted by a former choir-member. During the early 1970s the vicar, the Rev. Alan Taylor, often sensed a presence in the building. He would form an impression of an old man with a shock of white hair, wearing a dark-green cassock. On talking to an old lady about a year later, he found that the old man fitted the description of a choir member at the turn of the century, during a brief period when the choir wore green instead of the traditional black.

THE GHOST OF PERCY LAMBERT
1970s
Old Brooklands Racetrack, Weybridge, Surrey, England

Tales of ghostly phenomena were reported from the disused Old Brooklands Racetrack during the 1970s. The ghost of a man in racing cap and goggles haunted the assembly shed. He is believed to have been Percy Lambert who was killed here when he was thrown from his car, which developed a burst tyre during an attempt to break a speed record. He was often sighted by night-shift workers.

THE FOOTSTEPS IN THE CHURCH
Early 1970s
Sheriff Hutton, Yorkshire, England

Joan Forman, writer on the paranormal and dramatist, visited the tomb of Prince Edward, the only son of King Richard III, in the early 1970s because she was researching a play on Richard's life. She was alone in the church when she heard the door open and footsteps approaching. However, when she walked back up the aisle, she found the church was empty and the door still closed. The only other person in the area was a gardener mowing the lawn outside.

THE BLUE LION HAUNTING

Early 1970s

The Blue Lion Inn, Cwm, nr Rhyl, Clwyd, Wales

This pub is said to be haunted by the ghost of a farm labourer, John Henry, who was murdered here in 1646. During the early 1970s the landlord, Mr S Hughes, often found the cages housing his private menagerie of pets opened during the night and the animals missing. Many people claimed to hear inexplicable footsteps at the old inn. Nowadays the function room here is named after the ghost, (a not unusual occurrence with haunted inns) and John Henry's name is used a lot in their publicity.

THE CHELTENHAM LADY IN BLACK

January 1970

Cheltenham, Gloucestershire, England

The ghostly Lady in Black that haunts a street here has already been exhaustively documented by contemporary ghost-hunters like Andrew McKenzie and Peter Underwood, even though she's not terribly exciting as ghosts go. Doreen Jackson was having a driving lesson when she had to brake sharply to avoid the lady, who stepped out suddenly in front of the car. The driving instructor saw nobody. She is often sighted holding a handkerchief up to her face, and is thought to be Imogen Swinhoe, a local lady who died in 1878.

MATTHEW MANNING'S GHOST
1971
Linton, Cambridgeshire, England

Controversial psychic healer Matthew Manning claimed to see and speak to the ghost of an old man at his home. Manning was 17 at the time and said the ghost constantly complained of a pain in his leg, and that he was also responsible for numerous signatures scrawled on the bedroom wall. Manning also tape-recorded noises of a dinner-party from long ago, including the belches!

THE HEXHAM HEADS
1971
Hexham, Northumberland, England

A very scary tale of the supernatural now. Two stone heads were unearthed in a garden at Hexham, and from then on the residents knew little peace. A strange shape 'half-human half-sheeplike' was sighted in the house. The children became so frightened that the family moved out. The heads were sent to Dr Anne Ross at a Newcastle museum. Although used to handling such things, she found her work with the Hexham heads disturbing. She took them home and woke in the night to feel a horrid chill. She then saw a black shape, six feet high, in the doorway. She followed it downstairs where it leapt over the bannisters and ran to the back of the house.

Her children also reported seeing the black shape, the cat began to react to an invisible presence and doors slammed for no reason. A chemist, Dr Don Robbins, reported that the heads contained a high percentage of quartz and believed that these crystal structures stored intense energy. The heads were buried but disturbances erupted in the same area. They have since disappeared altogether.

THE PHANTOM HOUND OF DARTMOOR

Winter 1972

Dartmoor, Devon, England

Spectral hounds normally restrict their activities to lonely country lanes, beaches or woods (preferably near county boundaries for some obscure reason), but one phantom black hound paid a visit to a farmhouse. The dog's visit played havoc, causing the electricity to fail, the windows to break and the roof to be damaged.

Dartmoor abounds with phantom hounds. One of the most famous is said to haunt the road outside the isolated *Warren Inn*.

THE GREAT YARMOUTH TIME WARP

1973

Great Yarmouth, Norfolk, England

Time Warps are probably the most unusual of unexplained phenomena. One such incident happened to an avid coin collector, by the delightful name of Mr Squirrel, who visited a shop in Great Yarmouth to buy coin envelopes. He was bemused that the staff wore

1920s clothes, and the interior was very old fashioned. It was also extraordinarily quiet in the shop with no noise of traffic outside, or on the quaint cobbled yard outside the door. He bought his envelopes and left. A week later he returned to buy some more and found himself in a completely modern shop, as different from the one he had first visited as possible.

The cobbled ground outside the shop was now covered in paving slabs and the staff denied selling the envelopes as they didn't stock them. Examination of the envelopes ruled out the era Mr Squirrel claimed the shop seemed to have been in, as plastic envelopes had only begun to be used in the late 1950s. This rather throws doubt on the time-warp idea and doesn't rule out the possibility that Mr Squirrel may well have entered a different shop the second time round. And old-fashioned little stores are not uncommon, even now. One thing I would like to know about this case is, did he pay for the envelopes in decimal currency? If so, it's hardly likely that someone from the 1920s would accept it as legal tender!

THE GHOSTLY CHILD OF TWICKENHAM
1973
Amyard Park Road, Twickenham, London, England

Amyard Park Road is now occupied by a supermarket and offices, but in 1973 it was a street of houses. No. 10, an old Regency property, was haunted by the ghost of a little boy in a white jumper and trousers. His footsteps were often heard, and the owner's son was once overheard talking to him in his bedroom. When questioned he described him as "that little boy who comes to play". The lady of the house was once sitting reading a magazine when she noticed him staring at her. He ran out of the house, but when she followed him the street was empty. The child wore contemporary clothes, but the previous owners were childless. His identity remains a tantalising mystery.

THE GHOST OF DYLAN THOMAS
1973
Cwmdonkin Park and The Old Boathouse, Laugharne, Dyfed, Wales

The ghost of Dylan Thomas is said to haunt Cwmdonkin Park, where he spent some time as a young man. Margaret Hopkins saw him sitting on a bench there. She was later assaulted by a shower of stones and twigs in the back garden. Margaret, who had known the poet back in the 1930s, said that the impromptu shower would have been typical of his sense of humour. Dylan Thomas is also said to haunt The Old Boathouse, a remote house in a beautiful setting, where he liked to work.

THE GUEST HOUSE GHOST
25 April 1973 and 18 October 1975
Penzance, Cornwall, England

A guest house had not yet opened for the season when John Jenson and his wife called there in 1973, but the owner agreed to let them have a bed for the night. During the night, Mr Jenson became aware of a female presence (other than his sleeping wife) in the room. Mr Jenson found it a pleasant experience, almost akin to falling in love he said! In 1975 Mr and Mrs Jenson stayed at the guest house again. Once more Mr Jenson woke in the night, this time to find a youthful 65 year old woman (how he knew she was exactly 65 I do not know!) in a nightdress standing by his bed, brushing her long grey-blonde hair. She looked sad and put her fingers to her lips before disappearing.

Two nights later, Mrs Jenson woke in the same room to feel her hand being clasped in another pair, which she said felt like those of an old woman. The owner confirmed that the room had a strange atmosphere but, for obvious reasons didn't want it made too public.

THE CROYDON STONE SHOWER

October 1973
Allen Road, Croydon, London, England

A house was bombarded with stones. During the course of this event 40 panes of glass were broken. The police were convinced a human entity was at work, but failed to unmask a culprit.

THE BORLEY HAUNTING GOES ON
1974
Borley, Essex, England

Long after the infamous Borley Rectory burnt down in 1939, the church across the road has continued to tantalise ghost-hunters, and many feel that Harry Price missed out on a golden opportunity where this old building is concerned. In 1974 raps, crashes and inexplicable footsteps were picked up on a tape-recorder left running in the locked church overnight. This is just one example of many supernatural occurrences recorded at the church in the past 40 years. Like most extensive hauntings, some of it is substantial, and some is just wishful thinking.

THE PHANTOM HITCH-HIKER OF BLUE BELL HILL
13 July 1974
Blue Bell Hill, Kent, England

A phantom hitch-hiker haunts Blue Bell Hill between Chatham and Maidstone. Maurice Goodenough, a taxi driver, ran into a young girl here just after midnight, who disappeared, and he described her as only about ten years old, wearing a white blouse, skirt and socks. The mystery may be more complex though, as the girl did not simply vanish into thin air. Mr Goodenough wrapped the bruised and bleeding girl in a blanket and put her on the pavement, but when he returned with the police, she had gone. Tracker dogs failed to uncover anything not even a bloodstain, and no trace of the girl has ever been found.

It seems unlikely that she was a ghost, but even so the A229 here is said to have a phantom hitch-hiker. She is a girl who was killed half way up the hill in November 1965, on the eve of her wedding but it's hardly plausible that she was the same girl that Mr Goodenough contacted. A ley line runs through this area and there is some speculation nowadays that phantom hitch-hikers follow the course of leys.

THE HAUNTED TOILETS
Autumn 1974
Dunston, Tyne and Wear, England

A cleaner on an early morning shift at a factory was unnerved by ghostly screaming coming from the toilets which were also known to flush by themselves. Other workers claimed to hear ghostly singing and a voice shouting "Maria".

THE ASCOT POLTERGEIST
Christmas 1974/Early 1976
Ascot, Berkshire, England

Here was a very interesting poltergeist outbreak which erupted at Christmas time, an active period for ghosts it would seem. Objects flew around inside the house including, on one occasion, an ashtray with the ash undisturbed. The family car, which was parked outside overnight with the doors locked and the handbrake on, was often found moved in the morning by as much as nine feet, and without a sound being heard on the gravel. Lights flashed both inside and outside the house, but the most disturbing phenomena involved the telephone. The poltergeist would often interrupt conversations with loud buzzing noises, especially if any of its activities were being discussed. The family said the poltergeist seemed to be good natured and was encouraged to further activities if any of them laughed at it. The haunting came to an end when the house was visited by Angus Macnaghten, author of *Haunted Berkshire*. Mr Macnaghten recited a Scottish prayer, used to ward off shock, and the haunting ceased from that day on.

THE GHOST IN TARTAN
August 1975
Salutation Hotel, Perth, Scotland

Scotland is prolific in buildings that claim 'Bonnie Prince Charlie slept here', (the same can be found in England, with Dick Turpin as the guest of honour), and the Salutation Hotel is no exception. Jack and Gwen Mott stayed here as well. During the night Jack woke to find a Scottish soldier dressed in green tartan standing by the door! Jack was incredibly nonplussed by such an event and went back to sleep. When he woke again a bit later the soldier was still there. This time he faded as Jack watched. Gwen was disappointed that Jack hadn't woken her, as she would have liked to have seen a ghost.

THE PHANTOM COACH-AND-HORSES OF EALING
1976
Ealing, London, England

A phantom coach-and-horses careers across Ealing Common and disappears when it meets modern traffic in the Uxbridge Road.

It was sighted by a Mrs Willis, who was sitting in her car in the area in 1976, when the black coach pulled by two grey horses thundered past her. The phantom transport is a relic of bygone days when Ealing Common had once been a coaching route.

THE GHOST OF JOHN KEATS
1976
Keats Grove, Hampstead, London, England

Poetry-writing taxi-driver Gerry Sherrick went to see John Keats's house. Outside the house he saw a man in 19th century clothes sitting reading a book. Sherrick assumed it was a publicity stunt although the house was closed for repairs. When he returned with his family the next day, he told an official what he had seen. The official got quite emotional and showed Sherrick a portrait of Keats, looking exactly like the figure Sherrick had seen and sitting in exactly the same pose.

THE PHANTOM HEDGES OF SOUTHWOLD

1 February 1976
Southwold, Suffolk, England

I've heard of phantom houses and phantom cars, well now we have phantom hedges. A man claimed to see two of them near his home. He grasped one of them, and although he said it looked solid, he could feel nothing.

THE HAUNTED NURSING HOME

1977 and 1990
Thames Ditton, Surrey, England

A nursing home for the elderly here is called *The Home of Compassion* a name dating from its previous incarnation when it had been the residence of an order of Benedictine nuns. The last nun died in 1976 and it is possible that she may now haunt the home. In February 1990 a member of the staff, Elizabeth Gadd, saw an apparition of a woman in a grey habit in a corridor leading to the kitchen. The ghost walked right through her and Elizabeth admitted to being terrified by her experience. A few years earlier in 1977, church warden Derek Potts saw a nun walking out of the chapel and she waved at him, as though to tell him not to go in and to be silent.

A phantom dog is also said to haunt one of the wards. One patient asked for it to be removed from her bed, but no dog was there. The patient died soon after and this spectral hound, like so many all over Britain, is regarded as an omen of death. Cheerful thought.

THE ENFIELD POLTERGEIST
31 August 1977/September 1978
Enfield, London, England

This was a poltergeist outbreak which attracted considerable attention from the world's press at the time. A council house was thrown into chaos as stones were thrown, bedclothes were twisted violently, furniture was moved, cemented pipework was pulled out of the wall, and the children were even lifted into the air by an unseen force. Toilets were flushed, electronic equipment failed, books flew off shelves and footsteps were heard. The apparition of a grey-haired old lady, an old man and a child were seen. The epicentre of the activity seemed to be 12 year old Janet Harper who was experiencing menstruation for the first time at the start of the haunting. (Janet Harper was not her real name, but a pseudonym given to her by Guy Lyon Playfair who investigated and wrote about the case in his book *This House is Haunted*). After the children had gone to bed on 31 August 1977, their beds moved up and down violently, although their mother wasn't sure if they were making the whole thing up.

Janet, who often moved whilst she was asleep, was once hauled downstairs and on another occasion was found sleeping on top of a large radio! She often felt as though she was being choked and dubious obscene and objectional language was heard issuing from her mouth. A sofa was photographed flying across the room. Two *Daily Mirror* reporters kept vigil and noted that a chair had been thrown across an empty room whilst they were standing outside the door. Janet was frequently spun round violently by an unseen force, yet she stayed smiling throughout the chaos. This attitude has led to speculations about her involvement in the haunting. Not only had the haunting made her the centre of attention, but the family were visited by Matthew Manning, a flamboyant psychic, and Janet may have been impressed with the amount of attention and fuss he received wherever he went and decided to emulate his example.

Psychic investigator Maurice Grosse's involvement in the case could be seen to look slightly dubious too under some lights, for he seemed to believe that the poltergeist was his deceased daughter trying to attract his attention. Enfield is one of the most documented poltergeist attacks ever, and yet it is still far from conclusive.

When SPR researchers Anita Gregory and John Beloff visited the house, the haunting had been going on for several months, but both stated that they had seen nothing but trickery. Many times, Gregory reported, Janet would produce loud noises from her room and would be found sitting on the floor. Matters weren't helped by the fact that the girl now banned anyone from coming into her room. A video camera secreted in an upstairs room caught Janet trying to bend spoons and metal bars, and bouncing up and down on her bed.

In spite of all this, it must be borne in mind that over 1500 paranormal events were recorded, which frankly makes it implausible that Janet could have faked every single one of them. What does seem likely is that the poltergeist activity was genuine at the start, but descended into trickery when one silly little girl got more attention than was good for her. The phenomena was witnessed by investigators, the police, members of the media as well as the family itself.

Some of the haunting was also caught on film and tape, (one tape-recording of the mayhem caused by the poltergeist concludes with one of the family wearily offering to make a cup of tea, how very English!), and one of Janet's levitations was captured for posterity on a series of photographs. Whatever the controversies of the case and surrounding the people involved, it should still be respected.

THE HOODED SPECTRE OF SWINTON

29 November 1977

Swinton, Borders, Scotland

Ghosts sometimes make a habit of stepping out in front of cars and scaring unsuspecting motorists. One such character, a black hooded figure, performed this trick near Swinton. He disappeared when the vehicle ran into him.

THE PHANTOM HOUND OF SOMERSET

6 January 1978

nr Exford, Somerset, England

A phantom white dog haunts this area. He is said to be a harbinger of doom and is distinguishable by his red eyes. He was sighted by a couple here on 6 January 1978. It is said to be fatal if the dog looks at you, and this he did to this particular couple, casting baleful looks at them as they nervously drove past him on their way down into the village. The male partner of the couple died later that year, which some think lends weight to the doom theory.

THE PHANTOM FARMHOUSE
21 September 1978
nr Bridgnorth, Shropshire, England

A phantom ruined building was sighted by a couple out walking near Bridgnorth. Mr and Mrs Bull were walking down a country lane when they saw a sign to 'Boldings Farm', which turned out to be a red-brick building in ruins. They looked away for a few seconds and when they looked again it had disappeared completely. Ordnance Survey maps dating as far back as 1842 revealed that no such building had stood in the area, then or since

THE PHANTOM WELLINGTON BOMBER
1979
The Towy Valley, Dyfed, Wales

For a change from the usual kind of phantom object we now have a ghostly Wellington bomber, which was sighted by several people as it flew between Llandeilo and Llandovery. It was seen on two occasions, and all the witnesses noted that it made no noise whatsoever. The only Wellington bomber left in Britain is kept in the RAF Museum at Hendon.

THE GHOST FROM THE 21ST CENTURY

Summer 1979

25a Regent Terrace, Edinburgh, Scotland

Four students living in the basement flat of a Georgian building claimed to be disturbed by a brusque disembodied voice in the kitchen, a baby crying and heavy breathing. Watches and rings would vanish and reappear elsewhere. An invisible cat jumped on the beds, and the real cat would refuse to enter the building for days on end. Heavy footsteps were heard stamping down the hall to the living room, and doors were slammed. A seance held in July elicited the information that the flat was haunted by someone from the 21st century who had become trapped in the wrong time zone! The night sounds of general mayhem came from the kitchen, but in the morning nothing was found out of place. The students moved out in August.

THE GHOSTLY MONKS OF ST ANDREWS

Autumn 1979

University of St Andrews, Fife, Scotland

Ghostly monks were sighted at the university. Students said three monks were seen walking ten feet above ground level across the playing fields at night. I often find university ghosts do not bear close analysis though, and such cases should be approached with extreme caution!

THE READING POLTERGEIST

Late 1979/1981

Reading, Berkshire, England

The home of Mrs Adams, who was in her 80s, and her 50 year old daughter Pauline played host to a very energetic poltergeist for two years. The haunting gradually seemed to get more and more violent. Television sets were destroyed, the women were bombarded with their best china, the bathroom was flooded, and Pauline had her holiday savings completely shredded. The family experienced some very unique phenomena. For instance, on one occasion Mrs Adams's grandson 17 year old Stephen was stripped of all his clothes by some unseen entity as he stood in the living room! A friend who visited was hit on the head with a packet of butter, and old Mrs Adams was bashed with a tablet bottle.

Priests and mediums failed to calm the entity for long, and the two women had to move to escape it.

THE GHOSTLY HELPING HAND

26 September 1982

The West Country, England

An anonymous family lived in a 17th century farmhouse, which at one time had had a chapel in the grounds (one of the outbuildings was still called *The Chapel*). On Sunday 26 September, the owner and one of his daughters were returning home from church at mid-day when they saw someone leave the house, walk across the yard and enter 'The Chapel'. They thought it was the owner's wife, but when they reached the building they found the door was locked and no one was inside. The owner's wife was in fact found in the kitchen, and she said she hadn't left the house. This didn't surprise anyone in the family very much. For a long while they had been aware of a 'presence' in the house, and vague forms had been sighted.

They believed it was the ghost of a female domestic servant, and on one occasion she had tried to help the owner's wife put her coat on! The mystery was complicated further by the fact that the front door, from which the figure had left the house, was kept locked because no one was able to open it. Shortly after the sighting they arranged for a locksmith to visit, but before he got there the door was found to open of its own accord. Everyone thought the ghost was merely trying to be helpful.

THE GHOST OF A YOUNG MOTHER
1983
North Wales

An elderly couple informed the Rev. J Aelwyn Roberts that their house was cold and depressing, and that a particular spot at the top of the stairs seemed to be the focal point for the phenomena. The feeling was so intense that after a month, the couple moved downstairs as they couldn't face the trauma of going up to bed and they believed that the 'ghost' had 'taken over' the first floor. Elwyn Roberts, a psychic with whom the ghostbusting Reverend often worked, confirmed the old couple's story, saying that he had seen a ghost crying and sobbing whilst protesting she had not killed her baby. She was an unmarried mother called Margaret Ellis who had been around in 1836. The baby's father was Ernest Johnson who arranged for two tramps to kill the child by throwing it down the stairs.

Local gossip refused to believe this story though, and accused Margaret of murdering the child herself. Margaret died on 27 March 1873, at the age of 76. The ghostbusters reassured Margaret that they believed her story and from then on the haunting ceased.

THE COMPUTER GHOST

November 1984

Doddleston, Cheshire, England

A cottage allegedly saw the first use of a computer by a ghost! Ken Webster was in the process of having the cottage renovated when poems began appearing on his computer. The poems were written in a kind of Merrie Olde England way, and the writer accused Webster of stealing his house. The ghost was apparently a man from the 16th century. Bizarre.

THE IVYBRIDGE POLTERGEIST

November 1984

Ivybridge, Devon, England

A council house here was inflicted with a poltergeist outbreak. The usual bumps and creaks were enlivened by strange smells, screaming, footsteps and vague apparitions.

THE HOSPITAL HAUNTING
mid-1980s
Wycombe General Hospital,
High Wycombe, Buckinghamshire, England

For several years the bell in a certain room at the hospital had a habit of inexplicably ringing at night. One woman, who was in the maternity unit having her second son, heard this phenomenon in July 1986. The room at the time was used as a patients dining-room, and after it had rung five or six times, the janitor was sent by the nurses to deal with it but he came back saying that the room was empty. At one time the room had been used as the children's nursery and the same mystifying bell-ringing had occurred, even after the wiring had been fully checked. The nursery was moved, and from then on the nurses ignored the bell, which continued to ring eerily from the empty room in the middle of the night.

THE OLD MAN WITH HIS LAMP
mid-1980s
Essex, England

On a dark evening around 6 o'clock, a woman was travelling on a train between Barking and Upminster. When the train slowed down the witness noticed a little old man in an old-fashioned waistcoat, standing by the track and looking very anxious indeed. She later found that the arch and wall he had been standing next to, didn't exist. From his anxious expression it sounds like he was as surprised by the encounter as she was. An example of two time zones overlapping perhaps?

THE BULL'S HEAD HAUNTING
1985
Bull's Head, Swinton, Greater Manchester, England

In January 1985 Richard and Pamela Flammerty took over the Bull's Head pub. The following month Pamela was doing the accounts in the office next to the cellar, when she heard a scraping noise behind her. Turning round, she saw a stool moving by itself across the floor. Later one afternoon when the pub was shut, her son ran upstairs to say he had seen a man in a blue jumper in the empty bar but no one was there. On another occasion when Pamela and Richard were walking along the upstairs corridor one night, all the light bulbs went out one by one. They locked their bedroom door that night, and in the morning found that every light in the building had been switched on.

Footsteps were heard the following night, as though someone was walking on a stone floor, not the existing wooden boards. On Easter Sunday a male family friend and Pamela's stepfather decided to hold an all-night vigil in the cellar. Later that night Pamela and Richard were unnerved to hear screaming coming from the vault. The friend was making the noise and the stepfather was lying unconscious at the bottom of the steps. The couple explained that the light had suddenly gone out and when the stepfather had dashed for the steps he was grabbed on the shoulder by someone, causing him to trip over a beer-barrel. The telephone was also tampered with and found left off the hook.

The family left the pub, and the haunting has apparently continued, but in a more benign fashion.

In 1987 a barmaid claimed to see a figure, resembling

a monk, on the stairs. A hooded monkish figure has also been seen in the cellar and the current landlady's dog refuses to go down there.

THE VOICE ON THE TAPE
August 1986
Kilnhurst, Yorkshire, England

One day Dawn Deardon, 13, wanted to listen to a tape-recording made of herself when she was seven. The tape had been locked in a case at the family home for six years until then. When it was played back though, another child's voice could be heard over Dawn's, chanting"Born again never to die. Born again into your family". Dawn's mother said they didn't have the kind of equipment needed to superimpose one voice over another, and the tape had never left the house.

THE ROTHERHAM HAUNTING
August 1986
Rotherham, Yorkshire, England

Albert and Ivy Caldwell moved into a ground-floor council flat, only to be disturbed by scratching noises and sudden drops in temperature. One day, Ivy was sitting in the living-room when she suddenly saw the silhouette of a woman nearby but when she called her husband it disappeared. Council officers were suspicious, thinking the couple had invented the ghost to get another move. The Caldwells protested that they had been perfectly happy with the flat, but the ghost had ruined it for them.

THE PHANTOM LOCHSIDE COTTAGE

May 1987

Loch Mullardoch, nr Cannick, Highlands, Scotland

Two members of the Lochaber Mountain Rescue Team, Donald Watt and George Bruce, saw a phantom cottage beside Loch Mullardoch. It was a two-storey granite cottage and they said they had it in good view for several minutes. As they got closer though, it completely disappeared. Although it wasn't marked on any maps, they heard later that a lodge had once stood by the Loch, but it was now under water since the area was flooded and dammed in the 1950s.

THE HAUNTED FISHING-TRAWLER

December 1987

Bridlington, Humberside, England

A fishing-trawler was believed to be haunted when the radar would go wrong sending the ship round in circles, lights went on and off, the cabins felt cold and a ghostly figure was sighted on deck. A service of exorcism put things back to normal, although some of the 'ghostly' occurrences sound like the results of atmospheric or astronomical events either or both of which can create problems with radar equipment.

THE CAVENDISH HOTEL HAUNTING

November 1988

Cavendish Hotel, Harrogate, Yorkshire, England

Two young women booked into this hotel for a typing course. One woke up in the middle of the night to feel a movement near her, as though someone was sitting on her bed. She saw a man, oldish-looking, wearing pyjamas and leaning forward as though putting on his slippers. She thought he was real until he stood up, walked towards the window and vanished. She kept the light on for the rest of the night but later found out that another girl at her workplace had had a similar experience at the hotel. She had been booked into the same room, and had woken in the night to find her bedside lamp lying several feet away from the bed and her thumb covered in toothmarks. She didn't see anyone, but sensed a 'presence' sitting on the bed next to her.

The hotel has changed hands since the experiences of the two girls, and the new owners are unaware of any paranormal presences.

THE HAUNTING OF SPINNEY COTTAGES

1989

Spinney Cottages, Rougham, nr Bury St Edmunds, Suffolk, England

The Arnold family were dogged by unnatural phenomena when they moved into the cottages in 1989. Whilst they were out on Bonfire Night a fire broke out in a clothes cupboard which caused smoke damage to the rest of the house. A few days later, Sarah, 17, heard a disembodied voice say "That was funny, wasn't it?" She thought it sounded like her mother, but on turning round realised it couldn't have been. On a separate occasion she claimed to be roughly pushed by an invisible force whilst standing at the kitchen sink.

THE LEICESTER WATER SPOOK

1990/1992

Netherhall Estate, Leicester, England

Frank Boulter, 68, his wife Doris, 70, their son Stephen, 38, their daughter Janet, 30, and their grandson Luke, eight, all moved into a council house in 1990, and discovered that it was haunted by a water spook. Water would appear on beds, chairs, carpets, and even on one occasion, on the remote control for the television. An inexplicable coldness has been felt inside the house on numerous occasions. When men from the council failed to find any cause for the disturbances, and the haunting got worse as sticky deposits were found on beds and chairs (and one visitor even found the gooey muck inside her handbag), the Boulters called in Canon Ken Quine to exorcise the house in November 1991.

Canon Quine saw the apparition of a dark-skinned, dark-haired lady and a goat, but was baffled by the activities of the poltergeist. The house has continued to be haunted. In July 1992 the telephone, washing machine, and video all stopped working. Mrs Boulter said the phenomena occurred mostly in the evenings and early mornings. Tests made at Leicester University revealed that the sticky stuff was animal urine, but not that from a dog or cat, so perhaps this is where the Canon's ghostly goat comes in!

THE THROTTLING GHOST
1990
Lochgilphead, Argyll, Scotland

Here Christine Brown, 21, and her 14-month-old daughter Helen moved into a council house, but they were to get little sleep for some time. At night Christine would wake to feel invisible hands around her throat and a weight crushing her ribs. Even when she swapped bedrooms the phenomenon persisted. It only stopped after the Rev. John Callen blessed the house.

THE AYE-UP GHOST

Autumn 1991

Agincourt Road, Buckland, Portsmouth, Hampshire, England

Susan Griggs, 42, moved into a rented house here in August 1991. With her were her two daughters aged 23 and eight, and her grand-daughter aged two. However, when they began to decorate the home, trouble started. Cups of tea were snatched from people's hands and hurled into the gas-fire, clocks were put forward several hours, chairs were thrown, the eldest daughter was pushed downstairs, the oven door opened and shut on its own, cooking smells were detected when no cooking was being done, and taps were turned on. When the local vicar attempted to bless the house things got even worse. The ghost has been described by a medium, Ron Pomroy, as a "miserable old sod", apparently called Percy and originally from the north, who had promised to always look after the house after his wife died.

Even more bizarre, Mrs Grigg's grand-daughter, little Jasmin, began saying "aye-up". A saying not used by anyone in the family. Percy is now known as the Aye-Up Ghost.

THE HAUNTED NIGHTCLUB

November 1991

Butterfly's, Oldham, Greater Manchester, England

A ghost was caught on camera here. Cameron Walsh-Bradshaw, nightclub boss, was called to the building at

4.30 in the morning when police alerted him that his burglar alarm had gone off. Mr Walsh-Bradshaw played back the security video and watched as the apparition of a man in a hat glided down the passage and into Mr Walsh-Bradshaw's locked office. The ghost was on tape for six seconds. The security system company ruled out the possibility of double exposure on the tape.

THE HAUNTED GALLERY

November 1991

The Cafe Gallery, Salubrious Passage, Swansea, Wales

The gallery has had a strange effect on anyone attempting to work there. The gallery's purpose is to encourage Welsh artists, offering a place for them to work, but few have found creativity flowing there. One worked in the gallery for two days and then fled in terror, refusing to go back even to collect his equipment. He said afterwards that he had heard footsteps coming up the stairs and then everything went very cold. Gallery owner Ron Banning is currently looking into the history of the building to determine why it should have such an awful atmosphere which on one occasion made his hair literally stand on end!

OLD NANNA'S HERE
1992
Ruislip, London, England

Mrs Marina Jackson claimed that her grandson Greg, aged two, could see the ghost of his great-grandmother who had died in 1981, usually announcing her presence with the words "Old Nanna's here". A photograph of Greg taken in the kitchen revealed him gazing up at a strange white blur. A photographic fault, or was it really Old Nanna?

THE CIRENCESTER HAUNTING
Spring 1993
Cirencester, Gloucestershire, England

The Cheltenham Psychic Research Group, which was formed in March 1993, carried out an extensive investigation of a haunted house here. Vague apparitions had been witnessed in the house and the sound of running footsteps heard. The Group sealed up one room, and whilst members stood outside they heard thumps and objects moving about. This went on for six minutes. When the room was opened a small teddy-bear was found to have moved at least six feet from its original position. A psychic, Morven Alexander, was called to the scene and he claimed that two entities were haunting the building, that of a mother and her little boy called Thomas.

The child had drowned in a local quarry and had returned to the house not realising he was dead. The aroma of violets was also detected by the Group in the same room. It was so strong that Derek Newman, the Group's secretary, checked that there was no violet-smelling shampoos or scents in the bathroom. The Group are currently looking into the history of the building to see if they can verify the story of the drowned boy.

THE BOAR'S HEAD HAUNTING

May 1993
The Boar's Head, Mold, Clwyd, Wales

This haunting is a good case to illustrate how some modern non-Christian exorcists work. The landlord, Kevin Biddulph, reported that strange occurrences had taken place on his premises. Inside doors had opened of their own accord, cuttings from newspapers and a black cardigan had disappeared and then returned a few weeks later, and a barmaid saw the apparition of a woman in a black dress. A clairvoyant medium, Barbara Allen, visited the pub with her assistant Alan Johnson, and a reporter from a local newspaper.

Barbara came equipped with her exorcist's tool kit, such as incense sticks, candles, pendulums and amethyst, which is apparently, according to Barbara, the only crystal capable of sending a spirit packing. She started her work in the bedroom of the landlord's 13-year-old son, who felt uneasy about the room and the pub dog was often found in there barking at the wall. Barbara recited 'Go in love, go back from whence you came' in Hebrew (this does beg the question of wondering if the ghost is going to understand you). The pendulums, which had been put up in various places downstairs to detect energy began to swing vigorously. Barbara went into a trance and spoke of a positive legion of ghosts, including a pregnant girl from about 1700, a man called William who had been beaten to death in 1642, a landlord from a few years back, and a girl who had hidden from a hated marriage.

Barbara took on the voice of the girl and raged that she wasn't going to do something. Alan Johnson directed the girl's spirit to walk beyond the candles to a bright light, which she seems to have done. The landlord's son now reports that his bedroom no longer makes him feel uneasy and the haunting is no longer active.

THE FIRST POLTERGEIST
858 BC
nr Bingen, Germany

This is the very first poltergeist outbreak to be recorded. According to the *Annales Fuldenses* a farmer and his family had a poltergeist which threw stones, pounded on the walls, caused fires to break out, burnt crops and in a censorious voice accused the farmer's daughter of having an affair with the foreman of the farm. The farmer was dogged by the poltergeist wherever he went, until eventually no one would let the poor man into any of their homes.

A GHOST IN CHAINS
1st Century AD
Athens, Greece

Pliny the Younger recorded the eerie experiences of fellow philosopher Athenodorous. Athenodorous had rented a house in Athens, which had a reputation locally of being haunted. Tales were told of how the dead rose at night, clanking chains were heard and the spectre of a hideous old man was seen. Disease and death were said to strike anyone daft enough to venture into the house after dusk. In Pliny's words "the place was shunned", and to prove that some things never change, "A placard 'To Let' was posted outside but year succeeded year and the house fell almost to ruin and decay".

However, Athenodorous was short of money and needed somewhere cheap to stay, and this house fitted the bill.

One night Athenodorous was working late when he was disturbed by an apparition of an old man in chains who beckoned to the philosopher to follow him. Athenodorous irritably refused and indicated that he was working. The apparition got quite annoyed (obviously not used to having people being so untroubled by his appearance) and rattled his chains in indignation. Wearily the philosopher followed him into the yard where the spectre pointed at the ground. Athenodorous marked the spot and then went to bed. The next day he had the ground dug up and the bones of a man in chains were discovered. The philosopher gave them a decent burial, and the haunting ceased.

THE VIRGIN MARY AT LOURDES
1858
Lourdes, France

The story of Bernadette of Lourdes is either awe-inspiring if you are a devout Catholic, or unbearably twee if you have no strong religious tendencies. But there is no denying the fact that the legend of Bernadette and her visions is as strong now as it was 100-odd years ago. Lourdes is now a Mecca for the aged or infirm the world-over, and it has often been seen as a last resort for the chronically ill, who pin their one last hope on a trip to the home town of a 19th century peasant girl.

Bernadette Soubirous was born at Lourdes in 1844. Her father was a miller who lost his job when an accident left him blind in one eye. The family were thrown out of their cottage and had to move to a vermin-ridden shack. Bernadette had always been a sickly child, and her appalling home life did nothing to help her asthma. For a while she was sent to stay with relatives in a mountain village to try and regain her health. When she was 14 she returned to Lourdes and enrolled in a free school run by the Sisters of Charity.

The day that changed the whole course of her life, dawned innocuously enough. It was a cold February in 1858 and Bernadette had been sent to gather firewood. It was in a grotto by a stream that the claimed to see a vision of the Virgin Mary. Bernadette was rooted to the spot in terror and took her Rosary out of her pocket for comfort. The vision beckoned her, but Bernadette was too scared to move and the vision vanished.

Bernadette returned home in a daze. When she told her mother what had happened the older woman panicked and thought that the girl was starting to hallucinate, and thrashed her within an inch of her life. Bernadette tentatively returned to the grotto the following Sunday and saw the vision again. She had to be carried home later in a trance.

The vision appeared to Bernadette a third time and told her to go to the grotto every day for 15 days, telling her "I do not promise to make you happy in this world, but in the next".

The locals caught onto the story and began to spread the word that the spring in the grotto could cure all ills. Meanwhile Bernadette was examined thoroughly by all the local dignitaries who pronounced her to be completely sane. Getting to the grotto was now a problem as the place was swarming with people all desperate to see the vision, and Bernadette had to be taken there under police escort. The parish priest was urged to build a chapel at the grotto but he grumpily refused to do anything because he hadn't personally received a miraculous sign.

On 25 March, the Feast of the Annunciation, the vision told Bernadette that she, the vision, was the Immaculate Conception. Bernadette naturally became obsessed with the grotto. She would spend hours there in a complete trance. On one occasion she let her candle run down and the hot wax burnt her hands. When they were examined later her hands were found to be completely unscathed.

Bernadette had become a celebrity in her home town, but it was all too much for the frail, shy peasant girl. In 1866 she asked if she could join the Order of the Sisters of Nevers. The Sisters took her in and Bernadette stayed with them for the rest of her short life. She was strangely reluctant to talk about the visions after that, and kept up this attitude until she died in 1879 at the age of 35. She was Canonised in 1933. Bernadette was an adolescent girl in poor health when she saw the visions. Her life was hard, living in squalor with parents who saw the strap as the only answer to their children's problems. She'd had religion instilled in her ceaselessly from an early age, and like most French peasants she viewed Catholicism with a superstitious awe. I have no doubt that Bernadette did believe that she saw the Virgin Mary, for she certainly wasn't a liar. But no doubt deep in her pious little heart she was hoping for a sign, for someone to come along and solve her family's problems. The vision of the Virgin Mary was an hallucination of her own ardent, deep down yearnings. The grotto became a kind of sanctuary to Bernadette, a place of peace where the person she saw there, smiled at her and gave her reassurances of a better place somewhere else. When the grotto was over-run with sightseers even that was denied to her.

THE STAUS POLTERGEIST
1860
Staus, nr Lake Lucerne, Switzerland

Lawyer Melchior Joller lived in a fairly comfortable fashion with his wife Caroline, and their four sons and three daughters. They could also employ a number of servants. In the autumn of 1860 one of the maids claimed that she was disturbed by knocking noises on her bedstead, and she believed it was a portent of her own death. Soon after Mrs Joller and one of the daughters heard the knocking noises in another bedroom. Several months passed and in June 1861 their son Oscar was found unconscious in the wood store. He said he had heard knocking coming from within, but when he had entered a "whitish formless shape" came running at him. Sobbing noises were also heard from the room at night. A maid began to hear footsteps on the stairs and her name being called. Mr Joller thought she was being overly superstitious and had her dismissed.

She was replaced by a 13-year-old-girl which obviously was not a wise decision with a haunting already in progress. On 15 August 1862, whilst Mr and Mrs Joller were in Lucerne, the children and the maids heard the sound of knocking in the corridor. They became so frightened that they all fled outside. They sat on the stone steps of the front porch and a fist-sized pebble landed between two of the children. At lunchtime they returned to the house to find every cupboard door open. These were securely bolted, only to fly open again. Heavy footsteps were once more heard on the stairs. The new servant-girl saw a white shape in the kitchen, and this time they all fled to the barn and sought refuge with some labourers.

In the early evening, when they had returned to the house, the maid saw an object sprouting little blue flames coming down the chimney. The fire it caused was doused with water. The sound of a spinning wheel was also heard in the house. Joller, who had been stubbornly sceptical until now, heard rapping noises on 19 August and recorded them in his diary. The next day he saw the kitchen door bow inwardly. When he pulled it open, he saw a mysterious dark shape and from then on, the poltergeist excelled itself. Doors slammed, bottles and glasses were bashed, as though with a heavy implement, and loud noises were heard all over the house. When Joller was touched in one of the bedrooms he grabbed at whatever it was, and felt a small childlike hand. In September an apple bounced around the house but when a servant threw it into the yard it bounced back in again.

On 6 October the apparition of a sad-looking woman with a bowed head was sighted. Later that month the family fled to Zurich and the haunting ceased. The next tenant denied the existence of any paranormal incidents in the house, which led many people to ridicule the Jollers' experiences. Joller died in 1865, a mere shadow of his former self. Scorned by friends, he wound up penniless in Rome. Shortly after arriving in Zurich he had muttered "now I understand" but nobody has ever managed to ascertain what he meant by that comment.

THE MAN IN THE CAGE
1865
Place du Lion d'Or, Lille, France

A English family called Pennyman rented the house for a year and were astonished at the low figure being asked. They were soon to find out why. One night they were disturbed by the sound of footsteps coming from an empty room overhead. By the end of the week most of the servants had heard the noise and were determined to leave. Local legend had it that in the 18th century a man had been imprisoned at the top of the house in an iron cage by his uncle who didn't want him to inherit the family estate. In the attic was found a length of rusty chain and some shackles to add weight to the story. The maids had also seen the apparition of a tall thin man walking through a wall in their room.

The same figure was seen by the children walking upstairs, a few days later. Another English couple, Mr and Mrs Atkyns from a house nearby laughed at their story, and Mrs Atkyns volunteered to spend a night in the house herself. By morning she was visibly disturbed, claiming she too had seen the ghost, and her dog had refused to attack it. In 1887 the house had been turned into the Hotel du Lion d'Or and some English people stayed there (presumably the French were too sensible, as the hotel had precious few other guests). They too reported hearing the sounds of dragging feet.

THE HAUNTING OF CALVADOS CASTLE

12 October 1875/September 1876
Calvados, Normandy, France

A very atmospheric haunting this. It happened at a remote gloomy castle, which was already groaning under the legend of how a previous owner had died impenitent and was doomed to roam the castle for eternity. What is more factual is that the building played host to a particularly violent poltergeist outbreak, which was detailed in a diary kept by the owner, known only to us a Monsieur X. Also living at the castle was Madame X, their son, his tutor and the Abbe Y, and four servants. Like all old buildings the castle had been prone to mysterious nocturnal noises for years, but in October 1875 things took a decidedly different turn. Loud bangings shook the rooms, and someone was heard running up and down stairs at superhuman speed.

The owner recorded in his diary that at 2 o'clock one morning everyone heard someone stamping up the main staircase from the entrance hall, followed by loud blows on the door of the Green Room. Even more sinister was the sound of a woman crying for help coming from the grounds. When investigated nothing and nobody was found. A month later the sound of a woman sobbing was heard all over the castle, both at night and during daylight hours. The Abbe Y was subjected to some unnerving occurrences in his room. His furniture was often found moved, his windows opened and books thrown off the shelves. One evening at about 5 o'clock, he was reading by the fire when a shower of water came down the chimney and put it out.

The poltergeist began to get very noisy indeed. It insisted on playing the organ, even when it was locked up, and galloped through the castle at night yelling "Ha! Ha!" in a man's voice. Monsieur X thought someone was trying to scare him out of the castle perhaps because they wanted it for themselves. He bought two watch-dogs, but they proved pretty useless, whimpering when they heard strange noises instead of barking. On 15 January 1876 the Rev. Fr. H L performed an exorcism in the castle. The haunting, which had been fairly calm for the previous ten days, immediately started up again. The family had a Novena of Masses said for them at Lourdes, but the haunting continued. Screams were heard and furniture was rearranged.

The family could stand no more, and moved out in September 1876. Nothing further is known of the haunting of Calvados Castle. It was sold fairly quickly and no subsequent owners have reported any trouble.

THE FINNISH POLTERGEIST
January 1885
Ylojarvi, Tammerfors, Finland

Efraim Martin, 71, his wife Eva, 77, and their 13-year-old servant-girl, Emma Lindroos, lived in a small three-roomed cottage here. For two weeks they endured a poltergeist outbreak, in which doors opened and closed, objects flew through the air, and a sheep was found in the cow-stall with its legs tied together! Mysterious voices were heard. At the of the month Emma was taken away from the house when she was found to be suffering from tuberculosis. She died a few months later.

THE CROATIAN SPECTRES
August 1888
Verasdin, Croatia

Doubtless in years to come Croatia will have plenty more spectres to worry itself about. But in much more peaceful days, several witnesses saw a phantom army marching through the skies led by a captain carrying a flaming sword. The montage occurred regularly over three days.

THE TURIN POLTERGEIST
November 1900
Via Bava, Turin, Italy

Poltergeist activity in a Turin wine shop included bottles being smashed, tables and chairs dancing about, and kitchen utensils flying across the room. The police warned the owner, Signor Fumero, that if the activity continued he would find himself in serious trouble. In despair Fumero called in a famous psychic investigator by the name of Professor Lombroso. Fumero took him down to the cellar where the professor witnessed bottles smashing and rolling about the floor. Lombroso checked for hidden wires amidst the mayhem, but found nothing that could count for a human agency involved in the disturbances. In the kitchen furniture flew through the air, and bottles appeared to explode in mid-air.

Lombroso guessed that the poltergeist's catalyst was Fumero's wife, a little woman of 50, who had a lifetime of neurotic illnesses, so the professor suggested that she take a holiday. Whilst she was away the wine shop basked in blissful peace, although Signora Fumero claimed to suffer hallucinations whilst on vacation, saying she could see people that were invisible to everyone else. On her return the phenomena continued as before, and Fumero made the interesting observation that the only bottles and crockery that smashed were the ones that had been touched by his wife at some point.

This could be a rare case of the poltergeist having two catalysts. Also at the wine shop was a young boy waiter of 13, who was going through puberty. When he was dismissed from the shop the haunting ceased altogether.

THE PETIT TRIANON TIME-SLIP

10 August 1901
The Petit Trianon, Versailles, nr Paris, France

The most famous time-slip of them all, although it is shot through with controversy. Two middle-aged spinsters and principals of an Oxford college, Charlotte Moberly and Eleanor Jourdain, paid a visit to the Palace of Versailles and claimed to slip back into the 18th century. Although it was a pleasant day both ladies felt depressed for no accountable reason. They said everything had a dream-like feel to it and the landscape looked flat, as though it was two-dimensional. There was also a marked absence of noise. They saw two gardeners in old-fashioned tri-corn hats, and at the Temple de l'Amour they claimed to see a man of "repulsive appearance" who directed them to the Petit Trianon. Behind the building they saw an attractive lady sitting on the lawn below the terrace. She was wearing an 18th century summer dress with a green fichu. Eleanor didn't see the woman, but both saw a grinning man leave the back of the house and heard him slam the door behind him. They discussed their dream-like afternoon back at their hotel, and Charlotte joked that she may have seen Marie Antoinette.

Nor surprisingly the possibility of the Trianon being haunted continued to intrigue them. On 2 January 1902 Miss Jourdain returned to the area. This time she visited the Hameau, the farm that the French Queen had created so that she could play at being a milkmaid. She said she felt "the old eerie feeling ... It was as if I had crossed a line". She saw two labourers in pointed hoods loading a cart, heard the rustle of silk dresses and women talking. There was also the distant sound of music. When she visited the Petit Trianon again with her friend in 1904, they both found that the patch of lawn where Charlotte had seen the attractive woman was now a rhododendron bush, many years old. The two ladies wrote about their strange experiences and it was published with the endearing title *An Adventure* in 1911.

Soon after they heard from a couple who lived in a house overlooking the park at Versailles. They said they had had similar experiences so many times they no longer took any notice of them. An English couple, the Crookes, reported that in July 1908 they too had seen the lady sitting on the grass. She was sketching something. When John Crooke tried to get a better look at what she was drawing she flicked the paper away in a gesture of annoyance. They too heard faint music, and felt a curious vibration in the air. Not everyone was so supportive though. J E Sturge-Whiting, a member of the Society for Psychical Research, tore their story to shreds, saying that they had probably just witnessed a fancy dress party. A large fancy dress party did indeed take place at Versailles, but in 1894, seven years before the experiences of the two ladies. Over the years many people claim to have seen ghosts at the Trianon, with the people of Versailles re-enacting their day-to-day lives from the 18th century, before the world collapsed beneath them. Two English ladies visited the place in 1928. They hadn't read *An Adventure*, but they claimed to see a man in an old-fashioned green livery costume. They asked him directions, but moved quickly on because they felt that there was something hostile about him. It was later discovered that the royal gardeners in the 1770s had worn green livery. When the women looked back he had disappeared. All witnesses claim to have seen people in period costume, and many have experienced an inexplicable depression whilst in the area.

Many have concluded that all witnesses may have seen a replay of the day the mob stormed the Palace of Versailles. Just before their arrival Marie Antoinette had been at the Trianon and had had to run back to the strong walls of the palace for her own safety. Such a dramatic event may well have stamped itself onto the place. It surely would be no surprise that the area of Versailles is haunted, considering the events that took place there. I found the palace, much hyped as the epitome of grandeur and beauty, dreary and depressing. The rooms were neglected, and the celebrated Hall of Mirrors looked in need of a good clean.

The whole place had a solemn and heavy atmosphere, in spite of being crowded with tourists. The ambience of misery that permeates the palace may not be entirely due to the lack of maintenance on it! Professor Joad, a keen psychic investigator who has also had his fair share of controversy at times, concluded that the two ladies had experienced a kind of time-slip, and described it as "the present existence of the past", in that the past is still very much here and amongst us. Professor Joad conceded that this theory was "beset with difficulties of a metaphysical character". Indeed. But if we could grasp this theory fully, we might be able to explain ghosts completely.

THE HAUNTED ABBEY
1911
St Wandrille Abbey, Rouen, Normandy, France

The Nobel prize-winning playwright, Maurice Maeterlinck, lived in the abbey at this time with his wife. One night they had guests to stay, a Russian actor and an American lady. During the night the Maeterlincks were woken by their lady guest screaming. She told them she had seen an apparition of a deformed monk. A seance was held that very night in which a monk called Bertrand "made contact". A short while later the Russian actor found a plaque in the abbey inscribed with Bertrand's name and the date AD 1693. Maeterlinck and the Russian carried out a thorough search of the abbey and discovered a small secret room hidden behind some panelling. In it were the bones of a deformed man. He was widely believed to have been walled up alive.

THE ANGELS OF MONS
26/28 August 1914
Mons, Belgium

Now discredited as a genuine spectral event, the Angels of Mons is still worth looking at to illustrate some startling psychic impacts suffered in that dreadful war. At the end of August 1914, 15,000 French and British soldiers were killed when they set out to overpower the German forces, but the survivors were forced to retreat under the bombardment from enemy shells. After the bloody battle, the survivors began saying how they had seen phantom soldiers from the Battle of Agincourt rushing to their aid. Other confirmations flocked in thick and fast, as troops also claimed to have seen winged phantoms. French soldiers reported seeing the Archangel Michael and Joan of Arc. British soldiers said they had seen St George himself. Nurses tending the fatally wounded reported that many died in a state of exaltation.

Arthur Machen wrote a short story about the phantoms, calling it *The Bowmen*, which was published in the *London Evening News* on 14 September 1914. Later he said he had made the entire thing up, but the story refused to die. In 1930 the director of German espionage, Friedrich Herzenwirth, announced that the Angels of Mons had been the result of movie projections cast on clouds by German aviators, to prove that God was on their side. Proof of this amazing claim never materialised. Whatever the controversies of this case, it wouldn't be very surprising if the soldiers had seen a vision of some sort, considering the extreme conditions they were under at the time. There is a theory that they may have seen the souls of soldiers killed in battle.

THE VIRGIN MARY AT FATIMA
1917
Fatima, Portugal

At Cova de Iria, near Aljustrel, in the parish of Fatima, the Virgin Mary appeared to three children, Lucia dos Santos, ten, and Jacinta and Francisco Marto, seven and nine respectively. The children said she appeared dressed in while and floated above a small tree. On 13 October a crowd of 50,000 or more gathered to watch the Virgin appear, as she had promised. She duly arrived and told everyone to say the Rosary daily. It had been raining heavily but suddenly the rain stopped, and the sun appeared through the clouds, giving off rainbow-coloured rays. Some in the crowd feared it was the end of the world and threw themselves to the ground. Mary promised them that if everyone behaved like good Catholics, and tried to convert sinners, then Russia would be converted and another world war would be averted.

In 1927, in accordance with the Virgin's wishes, the Catholic Church ordered the building of a shrine on the spot where she had appeared and in 1952 a film was made about it, *The Miracle of Fatima,* which was used as propaganda for the anti-Communists.

ELEANORE ZUGRUN
February 1925/1927
Buhai, Romania

One day, on her way to visit her grandmother, 13-year-old Eleanore Zugrun, a peasant girl, found some money lying by the roadside, and bought some sweets with it. Her grandmother, a lady at the grand age of 105 with a reputation of being a witch, told her that the money had been put there by the devil, and that she was now in his power. Naturally such an announcement had a profound affect on young Eleanore. The following day she was bombarded with a stone shower, and various objects were moved, including a porridge bowl which hit a visitor on the head leaving a wound. Eleanore was beaten and threatened with being sent to an asylum, whilst her father arranged an exorcism which resulted in broken glass being showered down on the family. The girl was sent to stay at a convent for a while, but the events continued. A heavy table was levitated and the nuns' clothing was moved from one cell to another, even through locked doors. Exorcisms were carried out and Eleanore was hypnotised, but it was all to no avail, the phenomena continued. Eventually she was committed to an asylum, but a psychic researcher rescued her and took her to a monastery.

There he witnessed objects flying into the air, and Eleanore being slapped by the invisible entity. A countess with a strong interest in the paranormal, Zoe Wassilko-Serecki, took Eleanore to Vienna with her and set her up in her flat. Eleanore was delighted with her new life, but surprisingly the poltergeist incidents continued. Objects still moved and Eleanore claimed to hear the entity speak. It also pulled her out of bed, filled her shoes with water, and scratched her face. Scratches, pin-pricks and bite-marks appeared on her arms, hands and chest. Harry Price went to Vienna in April 1926 and took the girl back to London with him, where he subjected her to laboratory tests. Eleanore said that she believed the activity was being caused by "Dracu", the devil. Price was interested to see that Eleanore would frequently leave out chocolate for Dracu, in the hope that this would get round him in some way. Price himself was convinced that Eleanore was producing the phenomena herself though, albeit unconsciously.

Another researcher, Hans Rosenbusch, put her under laboratory scrutiny in Berlin as well, and concluded that she was faking the entire thing. In 1928 Eleanore, the poltergeist activity now at "an end", moved to Czernowitz, in Romania, and set up a successful hairdressing establishment. The end of the activity coincided with Eleanore's first menstruation. She also went through a rapid mental development at the same time. The Countess believed that Eleanore had a strong sexual drive, centred on her father, and that that was causing a lot of the poltergeist activity. The phenomena was genuine at the start, Eleanore had been considerably frightened by her superstitious grandmother's assertions, but it probably wore off by the time she got to Vienna.

Suddenly, from being a peasant girl with guilty sexual inclinations, she was now much in demand with many people from all over Europe. Eleanore may have felt that if she didn't keep the phenomena going then, her fairy godmother, the Countess, could lose interest in her and send her back to Buhai. Eleanore must have greatly enjoyed her times in Vienna and London, but she was also a very mixed-up girl. The author and researcher Colin Wilson, has little time for the idea that poltergeists spring from the human subconscious, for he claims it is "preposterous" that a young girl would carry out self-mutilation. Yet there are many young girls, and mature women for that matter, who scar themselves with knives and scissors, for no other reason than that their sexual hormones are all tense and skew-whiff.

He thinks it is mad to suppose that Eleanore would

have scratched herself so violently just because she had a guilty fixation with her father, but actually it is a perfectly reasonable assumption. Sexual guilt is a powerful thing, particularly if that person has had a religious upbringing, and can make many people do things to themselves that may indeed seem preposterous, but which are in fact quite tragic and sad.

THE PASSION OF THERESA NEUMANN

began Lent 1926
Konnersreuth, Bavaria, Germany

Modern theologicans are happy to admit that stigmata is a psychological phenomenon but even so, the case of Theresa Neumann is not so relatively easy to explain.

Theresa was born in 1898 in Konnersreuth. As a young woman she worked as a domestic help on many of the local farms, but she constantly suffered from a series of strange illnesses that no one could explain.

During Lent 1926, at the age of 28, she had a vision of Christ's Passion which left her bleeding from five wounds on her hands, feet and side. Every Friday from then on, she wept blood or bled from the wounds. At Lent she would go through the complete Passion, writhing in agony and losing nearly a pint of blood. Doctors who examined her said that her wounds would begin to bleed as soon as dawn broke on Friday, and during trances she would speak in Aramaic, believed to be the language of Christ.

Yet what was most mysterious about Theresa, was her lack of sustenance. For 35 years no food or liquid, except the Communion wafer and wine would pass her lips.

For several weeks she was kept under strict surveillance night and day by a team of doctors, who reported at the end of it that she had taken nothing. Not surprisingly, after 1930, she stopped excreting completely and her intestinal tract withered away.

When Theresa died in 1962, she was a thin, ghostly-looking woman who had spent most of her adult life dressed in white and lying in bed. In my opinion, Theresa was probably the most incredibly spiritual woman with phenomenal mental and physical control. She could dictate whatever she wanted her own body to do and it would listen. She was a great mystic, but her gift did not come from Heaven. It came from herself.

THE GHOST OF HARRY PRICE
1948
Malmo und Lund, Sweden

The legendary ghost-hunter died of a heart-attack in March 1948. He had dedicated his life to psychic research but by the time of his death, his reputation was being torn in all directions over his controversial involvement in the Borley Rectory haunting, so perhaps it is not surprising that he should reappear as a ghost himself. What is surprising is that he chose to appear in Sweden! At around the time of Harry's death an anonymous Swedish gentleman often saw his apparition standing by his bed. The figure spoke in English, but the witness had only a limited knowledge of the language. He did try to photograph him though, but nothing came out on the film.

The witness had to go to hospital for treatment soon after and he described his ghost to one of the doctors, who was interested in psychical research. From his description the doctor recognised the ghost as that of Harry Price. Quite why Harry appeared though is far from clear. It does rather seem as though he had lost his bearings in the after life!

THE DIEPPE LANDINGS REVISITED

August 1951

Puys, nr Dieppe, France

Mrs Dorothy Naughton (pseudonym) and her sister-in-law Agnes claimed to hear a complete action replay of the massive Dieppe raid that had taken place nine years earlier, whilst they were staying in a house that had once been inhabited by German soldiers. In the middle of the night they awoke to hear the sounds of men crying, gunfire and dive bombers. The noises started at 4.20 AM and lasted until 6.55 AM. Mrs Naughton had also heard a much fainter version of the same raid the previous Monday. The women sat down and read local guide-books about the Dieppe raid, and found that the details of the case matched the timings of the noises they had heard. They both wrote down their own experiences without assisting each other, and found that they bore startling resemblances.

Sceptics have pointed out that the women could simply have heard the sounds of the sea, or airplanes, or a dredger. But Agnes Norton served in the Women's Royal Naval Service during the war, and she would have been able to tell the difference between the sounds of a wartime landing raid, and waves crashing on the shore and commercial planes.

THE HAUNTED CASTLE
1953
Wildenstein Castle, nr Heilbronn, Germany

This castle was, for many years, a magnet for psychic investigators. Not only did it have a fairly substantial haunting, but it had a magical atmosphere as well. It was reputed to be haunted by the ghost of Adolf Hermann Erwin who had died at the tender age of five in 1890. On 1 March 1953 Baroness von Lobenstein saw a little boy in a sailor suit in the kitchen of the castle, who smiled at her in a friendly fashion. The Baron showed her a photograph of young Adolf and she recognised him as her friendly little ghost. An American officer billeted at the castle in 1945 wasn't so lucky in his ghostly experience.

He was having a bath one evening when he was interrupted by the arrival in the bathroom of a woman in white. He tried to push her out of the door, but his hand went straight through her. He was so disconcerted by this that he ran stark naked through the castle in a panic! Other paranormal events at the castle include a wine glass moving by itself, sightings of ghostly monks and phantom music heard. It is even rumoured, in local legend, that there are goblins at the castle.

THE ICELANDIC POLTERGEIST
March 1964
Saurar, Iceland

A farmer, his wife and their grown-up daughter all lived on a remote farm, but it was not a happy household. The wife wanted her husband to give up the farm and live somewhere less remote, and the daughter was desperate to get married. All this frustration and resentment erupted on 18 March into a month-long spate of poltergeist activity, involving the movement of furniture and the smashing of crockery.

THE SPEICHER HAUNTING
1965
Speicher, Rheinland-Pfalz, Germany

An American military family were living in a house here, and for a year were plagued by the sound of ghostly footsteps. The family made the intriguing comment that the ghost seemed to have anti-Nazi tendencies.

THE ROSENHEIM POLTERGEIST
November 1967
Rosenheim, Bavaria, Germany

One of the most famous poltergeist attacks in recent times. The epicentre was a teenage clerk called Annemarie Schnaberl. When she wasn't sorting out her tangled love life she worked at the office of a lawyer, and it was there that the bulk of the haunting took place, although strange events had been known to occur when she went bowling with her boy-friend as well. Light bulbs exploded in the office, lampshades fell to the floor, all four telephones would ring at once, pictures rotated 360 degrees on the walls,drawers came out, documents were moved and loud banging noises could be heard all over the building. The telephone bill soared when the speaking clock was repeatedly dialled, supposedly by the poltergeist. (Some psychic investigators have taken this as an illustration of Annemarie's hatred of her job, with her subconscious wanting to know when it was time to go home). Another remarkable incident was when a cabinet, which weighed over 400 pounds, moved more than a foot. When Annemarie walked along the corridors the lights swung and gyrated behind her.

The Freiburg Institute, headed by Hans Bender, investigated, but found the phenomena would only occur if Annemarie was under stress. They also noted that the power supply seemed to drain when the phenomena was taking place, always during office hours, but they were also able to record the banging noises on a video recorder. The telephone provided some of the most interesting results. At one time it was noted that a nine-digit Munich number was registered as having been dialled four times in such rapid succession that only somebody with sophisticated equipment could have managed it.

Annemarie quit her job and the phenomena ceased, but this didn't stop a news team from invading the premises. They claimed to see a vapoury materialisation which formed into a human arm by the air vent in the floor. It suddenly flew to a nearby wall and crashed into a picture. The antics of the news team aside,

Annemarie's experiences were probably quite genuine, and the mental state she was in at the time would account for all the chaos that broke out in the office.

During the 1970s Annemarie Schnaberl was interviewed by a number of investigators. By now she was a plump woman who looked older than her years, and was living in Munich. She had known little luck since the Rosenheim haunting. In every job she had after that, everything that went wrong was attributed to her and her "spooks". To this day she claims that she still doesn't fully understand what happened. The investigators had concluded that the phenomena, particularly that involving the telephone, had been caused by "intelligently controlled forces that have a tendency to evade investigation".

THE DOWER HOUSE HAUNTING

(Date): 1968

The Dower House, Killackee, County Dublin, Ireland

Ghostly apparitions and a large phantom black cat were all seen on the premises of this house. Workmen renovating the building saw the large cat. The owner, Mrs Margaret O'Brien, was sceptical until she saw the cat squatting in her hallway. She said all the doors of the house were locked and it couldn't have got in by any normal means. Tom McAssey, one of the workmen at the house, felt a room go icy cold on one occasion and saw a locked door open. He called for whoever it was to come in, only to be greeted by a deep growling noise. He slammed the door, but it sprang open again, and this time he was a large cat with red and orange eyes sitting there. A shadowy figure growled "You cannot see me. You don't even know who I am".

Mrs O'Brien had an exorcism performed which got rid of the mysterious moggy, but other, less disturbing phenomena, continued into the 1970s.

THE NICKELHEIM POLTERGEIST
November 1968
Nickelheim, Bavaria, Germany

A four month poltergeist outbreak started here in November and it was a fairly eventful time Objects passed through closed doors and windows, some went missing from inside the house and were next seen falling about outside, and stone showers occurred in closed rooms. These stones were warm to the touch, as though someone had recently handled them, a not unusual aspect of poltergeist activity.

THE HOUSE OF THE FACES
Began 23 August 1971
Belmez de la Morelada, Spain

A middle-aged housewife, Dona Maria Gomez Pereira, found faces appearing in the tiles on her kitchen floor and voices were also heard in various parts of the house, muttering in Spanish words like "spirits", "poor Cico", "drunkard", "little grandchild", and "what will become of your life?". News of this sudden and unusual haunting spread like wildfire all over the world, and ghost-hunters flocked to the little house to see for themselves the scene of all the weird occurrences. One of the faces, which had flat features and a suitably astonished expression, was photographed. Other photographs clearly showed faces in the process of being formed.

Witnesses claimed the expressions on the faces changed over several months, and faces would form on the floor even when the kitchen was locked and empty. No one quite knows why the haunting should suddenly start the way it did or the meaning behind the ghostly comments. The best that anyone could come up with was that the house could have been built over a Medieval burial ground as the building stands close to a church. Some locals though have tried to link it to the murder of an entire family carried out in that area in the 17th century, by the Governor of Granada who was born in Belmez. The floor was dug up and human remains were found under the floors of neighbouring houses, which bears out the medieval cemetery theory.

'The House of the Faces', as it is now generally known, is one of the most startling and controversial hauntings of recent times. Accusations that the Pereiras faked the whole thing by using chemicals from a drug store, do not hold up, as the faces continued to appear even during the most stringent observation periods, and the voices were heard when Maria was not on the site. There is a good theory though, that Maria was acting as the catalyst and that she was able to mentally induce the faces to appear, especially as they became visible regularly when she was under stress or feeling unwell.

EUGENIO ROSSI - THE HUMAN TAP

November 1972

Nuoro, Sardinia, Italy

Nine-year-old Eugenio Rossi was in hospital when he discovered he had the ability to cause great quantities of water to seep through the floor. The hospital staff tirelessly moved him from ward to ward, but the phenomenon continued. Plumbers expressed themselves to be totally baffled.

THE SAD GHOST

1973

Dattelen, Haard Kaserne, Germany

Mrs Kay Anderson lived in Dattelen where her husband was stationed. Over a length of time she said that she often saw the figure of a tired-looking man in a long dark coat in her hallway. She tried talking to him in English, French and German, but the apparition remained staunchly uncommunicative. She often felt an inexplicable feeling of sadness around him. Mrs Anderson was believed to be slightly psychic following a head injury she had suffered in her teens. No clues to the identity of her sad-looking ghost have been uncovered.

THE PHANTOM HITCH-HIKER OF BAGNERES

January 1976

Bagneres, France

A female phantom hitch-hiker haunts a stretch of road near Bagneres. Two young men gave her a lift in their two door car. Because she so constantly warned them to drive carefully, one of the men turned round to reassure her that everything would be alright, only to find that she had vanished from the back seat. This seems to be typical of French phantom hitch-hikers.

THE GHOSTLY SINGING OF MONKSTOWN

1977

Monkstown, Dublin, Ireland

At the time of the full moon a man's voice could be heard giving renditions of *Danny Boy* and *Ole Man River* in the middle of the night. One person who heard it decided to tape-record the impromptu cabaret and noted that the raucous singing was preceded by a very faint little voice pathetically calling for help. It has since been deduced that the phantom singer is that of Sir Valentine Grace, who owned a house in the area, and who had died 30 years before. What prompted the outburst was the fact that a tree had been cut down in the area, and he had left implicit orders that the trees were to stand unharmed. Quite why this should produce renditions of *Danny Boy* from the old gentleman is beyond me, as is the eerie little voice calling for help.

THE GHOST OF MERI GENETZ
12 February 1977
Meritullinkatu, Helsinki, Finland

A party was going on at a flat here. The hostess, Mrs Pia Virtakallio, was walking amongst her 60 guests, asking if everything was alright, when she came across a woman in old-fashioned clothes who she failed to recognise. The woman had arrived with Prof. Erik Stenius, and although it was minus 30 degrees C outside, she had arrived without a coat. This strange woman asked her if she required any help, but the hostess politely declined and moved on. She later asked a friend why Prof. Stenius hadn't introduced his wife, but it turned out that Mrs Stenius was not at the party. What was even stranger, was that no one but Mrs Virtakallio could remember seeing the woman.

She thought little more of her peculiar guest until three years later when she came across a picture of her in a magazine. The woman was an artist called Meri Genetz, but she had been killed during an airraid on 3 April 1943! The hostess discovered she was living in her former home. Meri Genetz had had a rather striking appearance and would have been quite unnerving as a ghost, with her severe black bobbed hair and dark piercing eyes. She was perfectly harmless though, and it is interesting that during her lifetime she had maintained a deep interest in spiritualism.

Mrs Virtakallio also often sensed a "presence" in her kitchen. She was intrigued to learn that Meri's husband, Karl Wargh, had been passionate about cooking. He had died at the relatively young age of 42, and that, plus Meri's untimely death may have meant that neither of them were prepared to accept death so readily.

THE MULHOUSE POLTERGEIST
1978/1981
Mulhouse, France

This poltergeist outbreak was investigated by the Freiburg Institute for Border Areas of Psychology and Mental Hygiene in November 1980. At the centre of the haunting was Carla, the Spanish-born female partner of the young couple who lived in the house. She had had several psychic experiences when a child and often predicted pregnancies in women. On two occasions Carla found herself locked in the outhouse even though there was no lock on the door. Cross-like markings appeared on her thigh and on the floor under the couple's bed. The markings were also found on a slip of paper rammed into the camera belonging to Thierry, her husband.

The activities occurred at least three times a week and usually consisted of knocking on the windows, and the sounds of babies crying and animals wimpering. A table moved by itself, and bedclothes were pulled off the bed at night. Instead of cold spots though, as is often the case, this house had heat spots, reaching as high as 27 degrees C. even with the heating turned off. Carla once claimed she had seen an apparition. The first time it was crouched on the cellar floor and described simply as a dark figure which had reached out to her menacingly before disappearing. The second time it had appeared in the apartment itself and Carla, in her panic, had run right through it.

The poltergeist seemed to enjoy tormenting Carla in the way that most entities are violent towards their catalysts. Carla was punched in the stomach, had her leg pinched and scratch-marks were discovered on her face and arms when she woke up one morning. On one occasion she felt as though cold hands were around her throat, and the marks remained on her neck for two or three days. Items of her clothing would also disappear for months at a time. The Freiburg Institute put Carla under hypnosis and an entity called itself 'Henri' came through. 'Henri' communicated only in Spanish, which may account for his affinity with Carla, but his messages were silly and made little sense.

Thierry and Carla decided to move to escape 'Henri'. Whilst they were packing up their boxes a neighbour informed them that the previous owner, Madame Arricot, had frequently complained of inexplicable knockings, and doors opening and closing when she was alone in the house at night. At the airport as the couple were preparing to fly to their new home in Guadeloupe, Carla burst into tears when she found that all her identity papers were missing. It took a lot of talking to persuade the officials to let Carla on the plane. When they arrived in Guadeloupe, Carla found her papers under the mattress in their new apartment! Electrical items were strangely affected even after the couple had settled in there, and the T.V. broke down several times for no reason.

THE GHOST IN THE GREY AUDI
4 May 1980
Val d'Adige, Italy

A man was killed by falling rocks as he drove through a short tunnel in the mountains near the village of Val d'Adige, in the South Tyrol. The time of his death, 11.30 PM, was confirmed by the man in the car in front who narrowly missed being crushed himself. At exactly the same time the dead man's girlfriend's sister saw him driving past the door of her pizzeria (which he had left only half-an-hour before) in Val d'Adige, in his distinctive grey Audi. He slowed down and waved at her before driving on. A short distance away his father heard the sound of his son's car pulling up in the yard. Reassured that he was home, he went to sleep.

In the morning he was surprised to find the car wasn't there, and his son hadn't returned home after all. This is one of the most astonishing examples of someone manifesting their own image at the time of their death. It is certainly one of the best examples of a crisis apparition in recent years.

THE STONE SHOWERS OF AVERSA
February 1981
Aversa, Italy

The Italian police have their own method of dealing with stone showers. When an outbreak of such a phenomenon occurred at a garage at Aversa, they fired into the air with machine guns. Novel.

THE PHANTOM HITCH-HIKER OF MONTPELIER

20 May 1981

Quatrecanaux Bridge, Palavas, Montpelier, France

Two couples in a Renault 5 car gave a lift to a female hitch-hiker on the bridge. It was after 11 o'clock at night, and they were concerned about her being on the road so late alone. She sat sandwiched between the two women on the back seat. She was silent until she suddenly shrieked "look out for the turns, look out for the turns! You're risking death!" The other women then screamed as she vanished. The car had only two doors and it would have been impossible for her to have got out of it without anyone noticing.

THE VIRGIN MARY IN FORMER YUGOSLAVIA

began 24 June 1981

Medjugorje, Croatia

The Virgin first appeared to six adolescent villagers on a hill here on 24 June 1981. From then on she appeared to them on a regular basis, and by 1985 nearly 2000 sightings of her had been recorded. Miracle cures were also claimed to have taken place. In August 1981 the Croatian word for peace, "Mir", appeared written in the night sky. Mary's purpose, apparently, was to stress that atheists must be converted, and that more time must be devoted to fasting and prayer. Medjugorje was honoured because many of the 400 families living there were true believers, and a good example to the rest of the world. Photographs are said to show Mary kneeling in prayer, and the image of Christ on the hillside.

By the autumn of 1987 Mary was really hammering home the need to devote more time to Jesus. Perhaps a little bit more emphasis on peace might have been required though. Sightings of her have apparently continued all through the crisis, although naturally thay are difficult to substantiate.

BENEDETTO SUPINO - FIRESTARTER
1982
Formia, Italy

Ten year old Benedetto Supino could have been described as a human box of matches. He found that he only had to stare at objects in his home for them to ignite into flames. Everything in his house went wild. Electrical items played up, his comics and bedclothes caught fire, he only had to touch the pages of books for them to smoulder, and the power supply occasionally packed up altogether. Benedetto swore he had no idea how he had come to possess such extraordinary powers, and accepted them as a slightly inconvenient fact of life.

THE ROME FIRE SPOOK
Summer 1984/1986
Rome, Italy

A fire spook caused havoc at a Ministry of Social Benefits office. One of the disturbing incidents was when the skirt of a 19-year-old secretary caught fire and she suffered serious burns to her legs. The mysterious fires were always immediately followed by a gust of wind. Several fires also broke out inside filing cabinets, desks, safes, wardrobes and photocopiers and although a faulty boiler was replaced, the fires continued and forensic scientists could offer no solution to the mystery.

VIRGIN MARY'S ON THE MOVE IN IRELAND
1985
Melleray, Cappoquin, Co.Waterford, Ireland

People visiting a grotto at Melleray, Cappoquin, County Waterford, on 16 August 1985, said that a statue of the Virgin Mary came to life and gave them messages. It would seem that a mass wave of religious hysteria swept Ireland in 1985, as statues were reported moving all over the place, notably in Asdee, County Kerry and Ballinspittle, County Cork.

THE BLOOD SPOOK OF ST QUENTIN

1986

St Quentin, nr Aisne, France

A very curious poltergeist outbreak this, but certainly not unique. At the home of a young couple, droplets of blood appeared on the walls, carpets and bed, and red stains were found on their pillows, kitchen table, bedclothes and pyjamas. They were later analysed and found to be human blood. The couple were also subjected to the sound of smashing crockery in their kitchen.

THE UKRAINE POLTERGEIST

November 1986

Yenakiyevo, Ukraine

Like so many poltergeist attacks which choose children as their catalysts, this one centred on a young boy. The usual general mayhem ensued. Objects were thrown, fires broke out, light bulbs exploded and a refrigerator was turned upside down.

THE ROMANIAN MAN IN BLACK

1987/1989

Bacau, Romania

From 1987 until the execution of Nicolai Ceausescu at Christmas 1989, the people of Bacau claimed that a black spectre haunted the streets after the curfew. Many citizens who went out early to scavenge for food, claimed to be accosted by this peculiar spectre, which would leap out at them from doorways screaming and waving its arms. It sounds suspiciously like an agent of the securitate to us in the West, but many superstitious Bacau citizens firmly believed that the man in black was a ghost.

THE HAUNTED AUTOBAHN
14 October 1987
Germany

The Germans have their own ghosts of the highways and byways, one of which is a phantom small dark sedan car of all things. A witness driving along the autobahn between Baden Baden and Frankfurt watched as the phantom car disappeared in an explosion of flames and smoke.

THE HAUNTED SICILIAN FISHING BOAT
7 August 1989
Crete, Greece

As daylight came a fishing boat called the *Francesco*, from Catania, Sicily, began sending distress flares just off the north-west coast of Crete. Safely towed to harbour the five-man Sicilian crew related a weird tale of having been pursued by spectres all night. The men claimed that the "evil spirits" had caused havoc on the boat, and thrown their radio and navigation gear overboard. The boat was indeed in a mess, and the terrified crew refused to go back on it, even after a service of exorcism had been performed by three priests. The fishermen returned to Sicily by plane.

THE HAUNTED PALACE
1990/92
Linares Palace, Madrid, Spain

The 19th century Linares Palace was put under psychic investigation from 1990/92. The investigators claimed to have photographed 22 inexplicable blobs of light, and to have tape recordings of 70 different voices, usually wailing things like "Mama!" and "Forgive me!" (in Spanish of course). Other supernatural occurrences include an apparition of a crying woman in 19th century costume, locked doors flying open, marble slabs moving, and music playing. Built in 1873 for Jose Murga, the first Marquis of Linares, the palace haunting has caused quite a stir in Spain. A radio crew held a vigil, and the locked palace was stormed by reporters and citizens all eager to see the haunting for themselves. Security guards, no doubt hoping for a bit of peace, firmly deny any paranormal presences at the palace.

THE SAN GOTTARDO FIRE SPOOK

February 1990

San Gottardo, nr Vicenza, Italy

A small mountain village was prone to mass outbreaks of fire, with most of the 500 residents being affected in one way or another. Fuse boxes burnt, televisions switched themselves on and off, lights flashed on a locked car, and furniture caught fire. The mayor of San Gottardo, Lucio Donatello, saw his front door burst into flames and on a separate occasion his electric razor ignited. The residents began to complain of headaches, nausea and skin inflammations, and animals went off their food. Experts suspected a nearby US communications base of producing excessive electricity, but nothing has been conclusive.

North America

THE VIRGIN MARY AT GUADELOUPE
1531
Guadeloupe, Mexico

The vision of Mary was said to have appeared five times to Catholic convert, Juan Diego. On the first occasion he said he had heard a choir singing before dawn, and a woman's voice calling his name. He then saw a woman standing in a cloud of mist, and she told him that she was the eternal Virgin. On another occasion she instructed him to go and pick flowers. Diego was a bit confused by this as it was a winter's day, but he found flowers growing in a spot where none had grown before. They were discovered to be Roses of Castile, a type of flower never seen in Mexico before. He wrapped his flowers in his cape and presented them to the local bishop but when he unwrapped his cape, he found the coarse material was imprinted with an image of the Virgin Mary.

The imprint has survived to this day and the cape is now exhibited in the church shrine that was said to have been built here at Mary's request. A sort of Mexican version of the Turin Shroud. A likeness of Juan Diego is said to be seen in the eyes of her image on the cloth.

THE BELL WITCH
1817/1820
Robertson County, Tennessee, USA

Probably one of the most violent and malicious poltergeist outbreaks ever recorded. Prosperous farmer and Baptist John Bell lived here on a remote farm with his beautiful wife Lucy and their eight children. In 1817 their 13-year-old daughter Betsy found herself at the epicentre of a poltergeist outbreak. It started when John Bell sighted a large dog-like creature on his farm and he shot at it with his gun. From then on, the family knew little peace. Poltergeist activity broke out with a vengeance. It consisted of scratching noises on the windows, bedclothes pulled off, stones thrown, both Betsy and her brother Richard had their hair pulled (Richard said it felt like someone was trying to pull the top of his head off), Betsy also had pins rammed into her and the beating of wings could be heard inside the house. Gasping noises could also be heard as though someone was trying to speak but having great difficulty in vocalising.

Betsy was also slapped violently around the face. She was sent to stay with neighbours but the poltergeist went with her, and she was subjected to blows and scratches. For two years the activity continued, and every night the inhabitants were disturbed by some kind of activity or another. Lights were seen outside the house, stones were thrown at the children, and visitors suffered having their faces slapped by an unseen force. Sometimes the raps and bangs were so loud that the house literally shook. A strange whistling noise began to be heard and gradually the poltergeist started to get a voice. It started off in a kind of gasping whisper. It told them it was buried in the local woods and its grave had been disturbed. It also told them it was "a spirit from everywhere, Heaven, Hell, the Earth. I'm in the air, in houses, any place at any time. I've been created millions of years. That is all I will tell you". As is often the case with the poltergeists, it also tried to cause as much offence as possible, making remarks about "the smell of a nigger".

The Bells employed a little black girl called Anky, whom the entity took offence to, and spat at her constantly, until poor Anky's head was almost covered with spittle. During the poltergeist's vocal sessions, Betsy suffered fainting fits and often went into a trance. John Bell himself developed a peculiar illness. His tongue swelled making it difficult for him to eat. The poltergeist told John (whom it referred to disparagingly as "Old Jack Bell") that he would be tormented for the rest of his life. It also, like most poltergeists, enjoyed using foul language. Betsy vomited pins and needles, and the poltergeist joked that soon it would be able to set up a shop!

The entity said it was a witch called 'Old Kate Batts', and it frequently filled the house with the smell of whisky as though it was enjoying a drinking session. Kate Batts was actually a local woman married to an invalid. There was no love lost between her and the Bells, for she had once conducted an unsatisfactory business deal with John and continually threatened to get even. What was intriguing was that she was very much alive and kicking at the time of the haunting, and enjoyed making predictions, such as forseeing the American Civil War and the two world wars of the 20th century.

General Andrew Jackson, a keen amateur psychic investigator, visited the farm. His carriage wheels got stuck in the drive leading to the place, and he heard a voice claiming to be Kate Batts, saying she would appear at the farm that night. That evening Jackson heard phantom footsteps in the house. When he attempted to shoot the entity with a silver bullet he was slapped and driven out of the house.

'Old Kate' the entity, had a soft side. It felt sorry for John's wife Lucy, and when the lady fell ill muttered soothingly "poor Luce". On Betsy's birthday it materialised a basket of fruit for her. Betsy became engaged to Joshua Gardner, but he couldn't stay the course of being with a girl who shared her life with a poltergeist, and broke off the relationship. Things weren't helped by the entity constantly begging Betsy not to marry Joshua.

On 20 December 1820 John Bell died, having suffered for over two years with his mysterious illness. For three years he had been the butt of the poltergeist's anger. It frequently struck him in the face, pulled him to the ground when he was outside and caused his body to go into convulsions. On one occasion it all became too much for him and he simply sat down and cried. The poltergeist went into a frenzy of celebration as he lay dying, singing songs rowdily and pulling the bedclothes off the sick man. It was even rumoured that it had tampered with John's medicine. When the liquid was tested on the family cat after John's death, the animal died instantly. After John's death the phenomena calmed down considerably.

When John Jr asked the poltergeist if he could speak to his father, the entity refused, saying that the dead could not be brought back. It warned the family that it would return in seven years. Possibly because Betsy was now happily married and living away from the farm, very little phenomena was being experienced then, although the entity made a few half-hearted attempts at reviving its old ways, by pulling off bedclothes and scratching at the windows, but it was completely ignored by John Jr and his mother, who now lived alone. After a fortnight it said it was leaving and promised to return again in 1935, but nothing happened at all and Dr Charles Bell, the new owner of the farm and a distant relative of John Bell, passed the year in peace. The way the poltergeist centred on both John and his daughter has led to speculation that John sexually assaulted his own daughter and this was so resented by Betsy that she unconsciously raised the entity and caused her father's death.

It has been said that John Bell suffered enormous guilt over what had happened between him and Betsy, and was prone to deep brooding silences and depressions. Colin Wilson argues against the incest theory, saying that if it was really the case, why did the poltergeist treat Betsy so violently? There could be a simple answer. Many incest victims suffer from confusion and irrational guilt, as though they feel they have somehow caused the offence to happen. This often occurs to young children who have been abused by their parents. The incest attack may have caused Betsy to hate herself,and possibly blaming herself for her father's fits of depression as well as subconsciously hating him for what he did.

It may have been out of some tragic masochistic desire to be punished (for something that couldn't possibly have been her fault) that enabled the poltergeist to treat her so horrendously. This is all wild speculation, for we have no proof at all that anything incestuous did happen in the remote farmhouse, but it fits better than Wilson's theory that poltergeists always go for the head of the family in the most malicious way. They don't.

No one knows what the real Kate Batts had to say about the entity assuming her identity the way it did. Did she resent John Bell so much that she was capable of manifesting her hate into such a malicious thought-form? Her resentment, combined with that of Betsy's, could have been sufficient to create such an eventful haunting.

There are a variety of stories about the Bell Witch. The one I have just related, I think is most authentic, as it is based on a diary kept by John Jr. Others have the haunting centring on another Bell daughter, Mary, who was fancied by a foul-mouthed overseer employed by Bell. The farmer shot the man in a rage one day and the overseer returned as the poltergeist, but there is little substance for this story. Another version has John Bell engaged to Kate Batts before he met Lucy. Kate died after falling over and hitting her head on a bucket at the farm and John immediately married Lucy, which is when the haunting started. This too is perfect nonsense as Kate was definitely believed to still be alive at the time of the haunting, and married to someone else.

What is more interesting is that the haunting was said to enjoy a bit of a revival in the late 1980s. The current owner reported seeing the apparition of a dark-haired woman floating across the fields, and also that he had heard mysterious knocking sounds inside the house. Maybe he's been listening to too many local stories. Legend has it that a nearby cove, called the Bell Witch Cave, is haunted by ghostly screams, footsteps and rattling chains!

THE HAUNTING OF DECATUR HOUSE

1821 onwards

Decatur House, Lafayette Square, Washington DC, USA

At the beginning of the 19th century Decatur House was the home of Stephen Decatur, a distinguished member of the American Navy, and his beautiful wife Susan. During the Napoleonic Wars, Decatur made an enemy of Commodore James Barron, the commander of a US frigate, whom he court-marshalled for wrongfully arresting four deserters. At the end of the war Decatur went back to Lafayette Square and enjoyed a high profile in the local community. Meanwhile Barron was nursing an ever-growing hate of his old foe. He slandered Decatur so much that Decatur had no choice but to challenge him to a duel. On 13 March 1820, the eve of the duel, the Decaturs held a dinner party, but Decatur was depressed, and took to standing gloomily at a first-floor window, as if he knew he was going to die.

The following day, Decatur was shot dead by Barron, in a field near Bladensburg, Maryland. His wife was unable to bear staying in the house after his death, and moved out. From 1821 onwards the apparition of Decatur has been seen many times standing at a first-floor window, as he had done the night before his death, even though the window is now bricked up. The sound of a woman weeping, possibly his wife Susan, has also been heard in the house which is now a museum.

THE FOX SISTERS
began March 1848
Hydesville, New York, USA

To the sceptics this case has a lot to answer for. It started the entire carnival of Spiritualism in the 19th century. In December 1847 a Methodist farmer, James Fox, moved into a simple wooden house here with his wife and two daughters, Margaretta or Maggie, 14, and Kate, 12. The previous owner had complained of mysterious knocking noises, but this did not deter Farmer Fox. On 31 March the house was shaken by loud banging noises, but as it was fairly windy at the time this didn't bother anyone very much. The entire family slept in one room, and as the bangings continued after they had all retired, Kate exclaimed precociously "Mr Splitfoot, do as I do" and began snapping her fingers. The sound of snapping fingers answered.

Her mother instructed the entity to clap, and it obligingly did so. Mrs Fox communicated with the entity using knocks, and ascertained that the ghost was a 31-year-old pedlar who had been murdered in the house. A sceptical neighbour, William Duesler, was called in and heard loud knocks that vibrated the house whilst he was sitting on Mrs Fox's bed. He communicated with the spirit, and discovered it was called Charles B Rosma who had been killed for his savings by the then owner of the house, Mr Bell, five years before. He said he was buried in the cellar which was duly excavated in July, and human hair and a few bones were discovered.

Mr Bell learned what was being said about him and strongly denied it. However, the spirit wearily announced that his murderer would never be brought to justice. (In 1904 a wall in the cellar of the Fox's house collapsed and revealed a man's skeleton and a pedlar's tin box). A team of psychic investigators carried out stringent experiments at the house. The daughters were stripped and searched, and made to stand on the beds with their ankles tied together, yet the rappings continued. When the girls were sent to stay with relatives, the noises followed them. The girls eldest sister, Leah, took them to her home in Rochester for the sole purpose of commercially exploiting what was obviously now a poltergeist phenomenon. Tables moved by themselves and musical instruments were played by unseen forces. Leah rented a public hall to demonstrate her sisters abilities, and the Fox girls were mobbed by an excessively curious audience. They toured cities all over America, for Leah had a talent for showmanship and made the seances even more dramatic. One of her favourite turns was to produce the ghost of Benjamin Franklin. Legendary showman P T Barnum exhibited them in New York City, and for a while the girls enjoyed a comfortable lifestyle living at the home of the editor of *The Tribune*.

A wave of Spiritualism swept the world, in something akin to a mania. But several years later it was dealt a staggering blow. In 1888 the Fox sisters, now middle-aged widows, both with a drink problem and disillusioned with the entire Spiritualist movement, announced that their whole story was a gigantic fraud. Kate's children had been taken into care because of her alcoholism, Maggie had suicidal tendencies, and both were jealous of their sister, Leah, who was doing rather well. At seances she produced 'apparitions', which were welcomed by her eager audience. Maggie and Kate decided to get their own back on her, and what better way than to denounce her livelihood as a fraud?

Maggie announced that Spiritualism was an evil,

characterised by sexual licentiousness and claimed that she had caused the knockings in the family home by clicking her big toe. She demonstrated this accomplishment and, although it was nothing like the noises that had been heard (how can a clicking toe cause a house to vibrate, one asks?) it was sufficient to throw doubt on the entire Spiritualist movement. Confirmed believers felt betrayed and booed her off stage. However, Maggie and Kate made 1500 dollars out of their confessions, which they both spent entirely on drink. They died in poverty a few years later, both within a short time of each other. Maggie recanted her confession towards the end, but the damage had been done.

In 1955 the Hydesville home of the Fox sisters was gutted by fire, but in 1968 it was rebuilt and opened as a tourist attraction.

To anyone who examines the case thoroughly, the sisters 'confession' may seem highly dubious. Out of all the phenomena recorded at the family home, it is highly unlikely that it was all caused by Maggie clicking her big toe!

THE STRATFORD SEANCE

began March 1850

Stratford, Connecticut, USA

The Rev. Phelps, a man with an insatiable appetite for the paranormal, held a seance to try and see if he could locate any spirits. Nothing made contact, but when the Phelps family returned from church one day they found various objects in their house disturbed. The Rev. Phelps stayed in the house alone that afternoon hoping to catch someone doing it, but he saw nothing. It is more than likely that he fell asleep. Soon after the initial incident, furniture was shifted and cushions and pillows were erected into human-like shapes. Sometimes they were arranged to look as though they were kneeling on the floor and praying, with Bibles opened in front of them, at other times they looked like corpses laid out for burial.

Objects also began to be thrown around, including a bucket which flew downstairs. A loud banging shook the house as though someone was trying to demolish it with an axe. Screaming was heard. The Rev. Phelps's two children, Harry, 12, and Anna, 16, could both have been used as the poltergeist's catalysts. On one occasion Harry was attacked by flying stones whilst he was out driving in the family carriage, and on another occasion his trousers were torn, whilst he was wearing them, right in front of a visiting clergyman. Anna was also pinched and slapped by an unseen force, leaving bruises and red stinging marks.

Glass was broken in the house, and dramatic messages were left on scraps of paper, "very nice paper and ink for the devil" being one example. The Rev. used rapping to communicate with the spirit. It told him to put his hand under the table, and when he did so he grasped what felt like a warm human hand. A well-known psychic of the time, Andrew Jackson Davis, visited the house and claimed to see no less than five spirits. Mrs Phelps took her children away for a while in October 1851, and the poltergeist phenomena ceased, never to start again. The Rev. Phelps estimated that the poltergeist had caused about 200 dollars worth of damage, which was a substantial amount of money in those days.

I shouldn't think he was allowed to experiment with any more seances either!

THE MASSACHUSETTS POLTERGEIST
1867
Massachusetts, USA

The poltergeist activity here centred on Mary Carrick, a young Irish servant-girl. On 3 July 1867, not long after Mary had joined the family, all the service-bells rang at once, even when Mary was in the room and kept under observation. On another occasion Mary was putting a tea-tray down on a stone slab when the slab suddenly rose up into the air and then fell again, breaking in two. Mary began to get hysterical after this, and raved in her sleep. On 18 September she was committed to an asylum. She eventually recovered and took up another post as a housemaid, but she didn't suffer from poltergeist attacks again.

THE AMHERST POLTERGEIST
1878/79
Amherst, Nova Scotia, Canada

Methodist shoe worker Daniel Teed's two-storey house was rather crowded. With him lived his wife Olive and two sons, his wife's sisters, Jennie and Esther Cox, his wife's brother William and his own brother John. In August 18-year-old Esther, a rather dumpy, plain girl, was taken to some nearby woods by her boyfriend, Bob MacNeal, who ordered her, at gunpoint, to have sex with him but someone approached before the dirty deed could be carried out. Esther was depressed for several days after this, crying herself to sleep every night, although she seemed to be more concerned at losing a boyfriend than nearly being a rape victim.

Esther seems to have been tormented with sexual frustration. She was prone to nervous fits, (usually a symptom), and had suffered from 'wet nightmares' about black bulls trying to break into her house. It seems that for poor, pathetic Esther, sex at the point of a gun would have been better than no sex at all. On 4 September, about a week after the incident with Bob MacNeal, scratching noises could be heard in her bedroom and Esther screamed that a mouse was in bed with her. Her sister Jennie rushed to her aid and witnessed a cardboard box moving by itself. The following night Esther's face grew red and her body swelled alarmingly to twice its normal size and she began to scream that she was dying. A loud booming noise was heard outside as though it was thundering, but nothing was found to account for it.

A couple of days later Esther's bedclothes were ripped off her as she slept and thrown at John Teed, who left the house swearing never to return. Her sister Jennie fainted at the spectacle whilst the rest of the family sat on the bedclothes to try and keep them in place. The local physician, Dr Carritte, was called to examine Esther's swollen body, and during his visit plaster flew off the walls and the words "Esther Cox, you are mine to kill" appeared on the wall above her bed. The doctor was also hit on the head with a bolster and raps and bangings broke out and lasted for two hours. The following day, Esther complained of an "electric feeling" running through her body. The doctor prescribed morphine for her but from then on the haunting seemed to get worse. He was hit by a bombardment of potatoes, which grew so violent that he was knocked across the room.

For several weeks loud noises abounded around the house and the family said they were so loud it sounded like someone was on the roof with a sledgehammer. Passers-by heard the noises and the phenomenon was reported by the local newspapers in great detail. Esther fell into a trance and revealed the whole story about Bob MacNeal. Jennie said that it was Bob's fault that the haunting had broken out, whereupon the poltergeist produced knocks as though in agreement. The entity when writing on the walls, would frequently sign itself "Bob". The house became like a circus, it was constantly crowded with sightseers, all wanting to witness Esther's antics. In fact, so many people turned up that the police had to be drafted in to help. A minister, the Rev. Dr Edwin Clay who called, saw a bucket of cold water which was standing on the kitchen table, begin to bubble as though it was boiling. He defended Esther against charges of fraud, and said that her body had received some kind of electric shock, which had turned it into a living battery. His theory was so popular that he was called upon to give lectures on it. In December Esther fell ill from diptheria, and during that time the haunting ceased, only to start up again when she recovered, by a barrel of wood shavings in the cellar spontaneously igniting.

Esther was given a job at a restaurant owned by John White, a neighbour, but the poltergeist followed her there. She was hit on the head with a scrubbing brush and oven doors clanged open in her presence and objects seemed to stick to her as though she was a powerful magnet. She was given special shoes to wear with glass soles, but they made her head ache and her nose bleed. The voices in her head began to threaten her with stabbing, and told her it would burn the Teeds' house down. As proof, lighted matches began to rain down from her bedroom ceiling, and one of her dresses caught fire as it hung in the closet. One of Olive Teed's frocks was also set on fire, whilst she had Esther in full range of vision. Not surprisingly, John White asked her to leave the restaurant for Esther's popularity was at an all-time low. A dubious-sounding Amherst resident by the name of Dr Nathan Tupper even suggested that she should be flogged, to "beat the evil out of her". "If a strong rawhide whip were laid across Esther's bare shoulders by a powerful arm, the tricks of the girl would cease at once". No doubt Dr Tupper had himself in mind for the "powerful arm"! In June 1879 a strange magician, Walter Hubbell, arrived in Amherst determined to make money out of Esther's 'gift' but the poltergeist resented this intrusion and threw carving knives, an umbrella and a chair at him.

During Hubbell's stay Esther had pins rammed into her hand and fires broke out in the house. A trumpet was heard playing in the house whilst the Rev. R A Temple attempted to perform an exorcism, and later a small silver trumpet was found, which no one could ever remember seeing before. No one in the house was safe from Bob's antics. Esther's brother, George, was embarrassed to find himself being focibly undressed in public on three occasions, and even the family cat was levitated five feet into the air. Esther told Hubbell he wasn't popular with the poltergeist but he wasn't to be deterred that easily. Esther was put on stage but when the poltergeist refused to co-operate, she and Hubbell had to flee from the irate audience demanding their money back. Hubbell went back home to St. John and wrote a bestselling book about what he had seen but Esther wasn't to be so lucky. The owner of the Teed's house, Mr Bliss, was concerned about what an effect on his property the entity was having, and asked Esther to leave. The hapless girl went to work on a local farm, belonging to a Mr Van Amburgh, but when objects went missing she was accused of theft.

When the barn burnt down she was also accused of arson, and sentenced to four month's imprisonment. During her spell in gaol the poltergeist activity ceased completely, never to start again. It has been supposed that the 'short sharp shock treatment' of being sent to prison cleared out the mess in Esther's subconscious mind. Although she was never to suffer from a poltergeist's antics again, she knew little luck. In later life, she became a fat, dowdy woman with a drink problem. The likes of Hubbell may have profited from her experiences, but Esther never did.

THE QUEBEC POLTERGEIST
1889
Quebec, Canada

Poltergeist activity erupted on George Dagg's farm here. It started most unpleasantly with streaks of excrement and manure appearing on the walls. The young boy, Dean, was blamed but the horrible phenomena continued when he was out of the house. Crockery was moved, windows smashed and fires broke out and it soon became apparent that the epicentre was 11-year-old Dinah McLean, the Dagg's adopted daughter. In November 1889 an artist named Woodcock, listened as Dinah chatted to the entity in the woodshed whilst it revealed it was "the devil" and wanted to break Woodcock's neck. It calmed down later and said it was only causing the haunting for "fun".

Crowds began to gather at the woodshed and claimed

to witness stones flying and a mouth organ playing by itself. Unlike Esther Cox's poltergeist this one was certainly not anti-social! The poltergeist rather enjoyed showing off and abandoned its ideas of being "the devil", in fact it began to sing rather pleasantly. However, it ceased its antics after only a short while.

THE GREENBRIER GHOST
1897
Greenbrier, West Virginia, USA

Zona Shue lived at Greenbrier with her husband Trout Shue. Zona was born about 1873 and in 1895 bore an illegitimate baby. In 1896 she met Trout Shue and the couple were married shortly afterwards. Zona's mother was bitterly opposed to the wedding, for she didn't like the thought of her daughter marrying a complete stranger, despite the arrival of an illegitimate child. On 23 January 1897 a little coloured boy, Andy Jones, was stopped by Trout in the street who asked him to go to his house and enquire if his wife wanted anything from the store. Andy went to the Shue's house and found Zona lying dead on the kitchen floor. The frightened lad rushed to get Trout, who then started acting in a most peculiar manner. By the time the coroner, Dr George W Knapp, had arrived at the house, Trout had carried his wife upstairs and dressed her in her Sunday best!

Trout was wailing and cradling his wife's head in his lap. When Knapp tried to examine the body Trout became so distressed that the doctor had to desist, and recorded Zona's death as "complications from childbirth". Trout's behaviour got even odder. He tied a scarf around Zona's neck and wouldn't let anyone touch it and in fact he wouldn't let anyone get near the corpse at all. When Zona's mother, Heaster, tried to wash the sheet inside the coffin she found it splattered with a red indelible stain and took it as a sign that her daughter's death had not been natural. She began to pray for Zona to return from the dead and tell everyone the truth of what happened and incredibly it seems her prayers were soon answered.

Zona appeared at her mother's bedside and said that Trout had broken her neck in a violent rage, simply because she hadn't cooked any meat for dinner. To demonstrate this, Zona's head spun round! Rumours were already abounding in the district about Zona's death and prosecutor, John Alfred Preston ordered an inquiry. Trout objected to Zona's body being exhumed, and said they wouldn't be able to prove he had murdered her. When Zona's body was found to have a broken neck and windpipe, Trout was arrested for murder. During the run-up to his trial the truth came out about Trout. His first wife complained that he had abused her, and his second had died in mysterious circumstances when she was knocked unconscious by a falling rock.

Trout was in good spirits in jail. He announced that it was his lifelong ambition to have seven wives, but he was found guilty and sentenced to life imprisonment. The killer was excused the death penalty on the grounds that the evidence against him was purely circumstantial. He died of an infection in 1900 at the Moundsville State Penitentiary, the only man to be convicted on the evidence of a rather dubious ghost!

THE RETURN OF LT JAMES SUTTON
1907
Portland, Oregon, USA

Lt James Sutton was shot in the head at Annapolis, Maryland, on 12 October 1907. At the inquest it was concluded that Sutton had got drunk at a navy dance and had shot himself with his own pistol. His mother refused to believe the verdict and told the Society for Psychical Research in America that she had seen an apparition of her son, in which he protested that he had been killed, not committed suicide. In 1909 the body was exhumed and it was found that the navy's findings were woefully incomplete, that several wounds he had suffered during a drunken brawl after the dance, had not been mentioned at the inquest.

After the exhumation the sightings of his apparition ceased even though no conclusion to the mystery was ever reached.

THE HAUNTED JAIL
April 1908
Asheville, North Carolina, USA

Prisoners at this county jail signed a petition appealing for protection from evil spirits and demons. They claimed they had seen ghosts "leering" at them, and had heard strange noises.

THE CALEDONIA MILLS FIRE SPOOK

January 1922

Caledonia Mills, nr Antigonish, Nova Scotia, Canada

A series of mysterious fires broke out here in a lonely farmhouse. It was the home of Alexander MacDonald, 72, his wife and their adopted daughter Mary Ellen, 15. One night between 5.00 PM and 8.00 AM no less than 38 separate fires broke out, and were witnessed by three neighbours. One, a retired electrician, said the whole house lit up as though a short circuit had occurred on a high tension wire. He saw blue flames shoot out of a window-blind, a patch of wet wallpaper and on a cardboard picture. Although he grasped the window-blind to extinguish the fire, he said the flames weren't hot and the hairs on his hand weren't scorched.

The following night 31 fires broke out, and the house was drenched with water as the family and neighbours continuously battled with the ghostly arsonist. Mary Ellen was put under supervision but nothing was observed, although it does seem that she was the catalyst. Living on a remote farm with two elderly people is, after all, not much of a life for a 15 year old girl.

AN INVALID'S POLTERGEIST

March 1922

Alva, Oklahoma, USA

Mrs Ona Smith, aged 23, was paralysed and confined to bed here in her cottage. She was often terrified by spontaneous outbreaks of fire, when blue flames would appear out of thin air. Nothing was safe from the fire spook. Ona's bedding, clothing and curtains all caught fire at random. Friends and neighbours kept a 24 hour vigil by her bedside, but could do little other than fly to the rescue when a fire broke out. Over a few days two mattresses were reduced to smouldering ruins, and a calendar and a shawl burst into flames. A new mattress spontaneously ignited in the presence of several witnesses, including a newspaper reporter. All witnesses stated that the fires seemed to start in mid-air.

THE CHAFFIN WILL CASE
1925
North Carolina, USA

Farmer James L Chaffin made out a will in November 1905 in which he left everything to his third son Marshall, thus excluding his wife and other three sons. In January 1919 though, Chaffin had a change of heart, amending his will so that it included everyone, and asking the boys to look after their "mammy". Chaffin told no one about the new will and hid it inside his old Bible. On 7 September 1921 Chaffin died after suffering a serious fall. The 1905 will was probated, and everything went to Marshall, for no one contested it. In 1925 another son, James, had a dream in which his father appeared at his bedside and told him to look in his overcoat pocket. Shortly after this he managed to get hold of his father's old overcoat and found the pocket stitched up.

He tore it open and found a note telling him to look in his old Bible. James rounded up some witnesses, the

Bible was located and the will discovered. The second will was submitted to a court, where it was contested by Marshall's widow. When she was shown the will though, she agreed that the handwriting was Chaffin's and withdrew her protest. The time lapse rules out the forgery theory, for why would James wait four years to produce either a faked will, (and everyone agreed that it was in Chaffin Snr's handwriting), or to produce a will that he knew about. From the details of the case, it would seem that Chaffin Snr kept the new will a secret from everyone, so for anyone desperately wanting to believe in life after death, this sort of case could well provide some evidence.

THE WINDSOR FIRE SPOOK

December 1941

Dominion Golf and Country Club, nr Windsor, Ontario, Canada

Bluish flames shot out of bits of paper, tablecloths, towels and curtains here. When the manager went to grab the telephone directory to call the fire brigade, that ignited as well! A sceptical insurance agent was questioning the manager the following day when a broom caught fire in front of him and on one spectacular occasion a tablecloth in the dining room was seen covered in dancing blue flames. No one was hurt during this brief but very eventful haunting.

THE MACOMB FIRE SPOOK
August 1948
nr Macomb, Illinois, USA

The fires on a farm south of Macomb began when small brown scorch-marks appeared on the wallpaper on 7 August. Gradually these ignited into flames. The wallpaper was torn off but then the bare wooden walls would ignite instead. Macomb Fire Chief Fred Wilson was embarrassed by the phenomenon, describing it as "screwy and fantastic". Although he couldn't explain it, he had to admit that a dozen witnesses had seen the scorch-marks appear and then ignite. Curtains also caught fire, as well as an ironing-board on the outside porch. All in all, approximately 200 fires broke out in one week and on 14 August the cottage burnt down.

The farmer's 13-year-old niece was put under interrogation and confessed, but many were sceptical as this didn't explain how the scorch-marks could appear in front of people's eyes and ignite by themselves. A reporter, Vincent H Gaddis, didn't believe the girl's confession and said "I'm certain I could flip matches at ceilings all day with perfect safety".

THE MOUNT RAINIER POLTERGEIST
1949
Mount Rainier, Washington, USA

Thirteen year old Douglass Deen was at the centre of this particular poltergeist outbreak during which time there were scratching noises, dishes and fruit flying through the air and pictures floating off the walls. Douglass's bed vibrated whilst he was in it and the bedclothes were pulled off, but when he tried hanging onto them he was pulled onto the floor. Scratching noises broke out on the ceiling, footsteps were heard in the hall, and furniture and dishes were moved. On 17 February the Rev. Winston slept in the same room as Douglass and saw that the boy's bed began to move. The priest asked him to sleep in the armchair, but that began to move as well. Douglass was taken to the Georgetown Hospital where he received medical treatment, and the St. Louis University where he received psychiatric help. Meanwhile a Lutheran minister, Luther Schulze, was called in to exorcise the farm.

He had to make 30 attempts before it worked. Whilst one exorcism was taking place Douglass, still in hospital, began to mouth obscenities and shout in Latin, a language about which he knew nothing. The message "go to St. Louis" was found inscribed on his skin. Douglass began to cough violently and more scratches appeared on his arm so the lad himself was subjected to an exorcism. During the rite he spat at the priests and his body jerked violently. But when he returned home in April the phenomena ceased.

This case is the one which inspired William Peter Blatty, author of *The Exorcist*. Blatty had been a student in Washington at the time of the outbreak and read about it in the local papers. More than 20 years later he turned it into a bestselling book. In the book and the film, Douglass's sex was changed and he was played by Linda Blair. The story was also considerably dramatised, with green vomit and spinning heads added.

THE FLAT ROCK FIRE SPOOK
November 1954
Flat Rock, St John's Newfoundland, Canada

A house was infested for a fortnight with a fire-spook. A doll, a dictionary, a box of religious papers and a sack of sugar all caught fire suddenly and for no reason.

HAROLD'S DOPPELGANGER
1958
Chicago, Illinois, USA

One day a man known only to us as 'Harold' was suffering a migraine attack. As he sat down to dinner he noticed an exact replica of himself sitting opposite, copying his every movement. At the end of the meal the image vanished, but Harold claimed he had similar experiences whenever he had a migraine attack.

THE GHOST IN EDGAR ALLEN POE'S HOUSE
1960s onwards
Baltimore, Maryland, USA

The house where the great mystery writer, Edgar Allen Poe lived and died is, apparently, not haunted by the man himself yet in 1949 the house was opened to the public, and from the 1960s onwards strange phenomena was reported. Lights have been switched on, doors open and close of their own accord, and visitors are tapped on the shoulder by an invisible someone. Most of the haunting seems based in the attic room and the bedroom where Poe's cousin, Virginia Clemm slept. Psychics claim to have seen the apparition of an old woman with grey hair in old-fashioned clothes, but who she is remains a mystery.

THE BALTIMORE POLTERGEIST

14 January/8 February 1960
Baltimore, Maryland, USA

So many items of household stuff were broken or thrown around during this poltergeist outbreak that the family threw everything out into the backyard in desperation! The house was lived in by retired fireman Edgar C Jones, his wife, the couple's son-in-law and daughter, and their 17-year-old grandson Ted Pauls. Ted was a strange boy. He had dropped out of high school and spent all his time reading science fiction, and writing his own newsletter. Everyone was concerned that this highly intelligent young man was hiding himself away and wasting his time. The haunting began when 15 minature pottery pitchers exploded at once on a dining room shelf, from then on nothing was safe. Mr Jones was hit on the head with a tin of sauerkraut and a table was thrown downstairs.

About a fortnight after the haunting had started, Mrs Jones found she could take no more and went to live with her sister until things calmed down. The haunting ceased without warning on 8 February. But by then the damage was done, in more ways than one. The Jones's home was constantly infested with newspaper reporters, and many sceptical witnesses accused Ted of faking the whole thing, but a plumber had a different explanation. He said that the hot air furnace was at the root of all the problems, and asked the family to open all the windows to reduce the pressure. When they did so the events came to a stop. This is possibly the first haunting ever to be exorcised by a plumber! Nandor Fodor interviewed the family, and concluded that Ted was unconsciously directing his mental power to cause the disturbances.

Ted was a frustrated writer, who was annoyed that no one was recognising his hidden talents. Fodor went on radio to say that if Ted was allowed to write his own account of the haunting, it might help matters considerably. This certainly worked wonders for Ted's self-esteem and ensured that the poltergeist wouldn't be allowed back. The Jones's were convinced that the plumber was to take the credit though, and the case remains inconclusive.

THE GHOST OF ALCATRAZ

1963 onwards
Alcatraz, San Francisco Bay, California, USA

With the exception of Devil's Island, Alcatraz has to have been one of the most dismal and soul-destroying prisons ever to be built. As such, it would be very surprising if it wasn't haunted in one way or another. Alcatraz was originally an army fort, but in 1934 it was turned into a federal penitentiary to house some of America's toughest criminals. Such words as "rehabilitation" were unknown at the time for the grim building was intended purely as a place of punishment, with escape an impossible dream. Al Capone ended his days on Alcatraz. He had gone totally insane, from a combination of syphilis and his incarceration on "the Rock". He was constantly threatened by the other inmates, so he spent his days by himself, playing a banjo in his cell or in the shower.

In 1946 a bloodbath took place when six prisoners attempted to escape. The attempt ended in the deaths of three guards and three of the inmates. Solitary confinement was the most feared punishment. In Cell Blocks 11, 12, 13 and 14 in Block D a prisoner could be stripped and shut in complete darkness for great lengths of time, only getting a proper meal once every three days. Since Alcatraz was closed down as a prison and opened to the public in 1963, guards and tour guides have reported hearing inexplicable noises, such as screams, whistling, feet running along the corridors and the clanging of metal doors. Men's voices have been heard in the hospital ward. The area around Cell 14-D, one of the places of solitary confinement, has felt dreadfully cold, even on hot days, and many people have felt "strange" there, although many have admitted this could merely be due to what they have heard about the place.

Banjo music has also been heard coming from the shower room, possibly the ghostly reminder of how one of the most powerful men in America ended his days as a demented and lonely outcast.

THE GHOST IN THE PICTURE
23 November 1965/February 1970
Haw Branch, Amelia, Virginia, USA

An old plantation house here called Haw Branch played host to a very classic haunting. A couple called Cary and Gibson McConnaughey bought the house in 1964. Gibson was already acquainted with the place as her grandmother had lived there many years before. Little did they suspect that their beautiful home was going to produce some unnerving phenomena for them both. On 23 November 1965 the sound of a woman screaming was heard coming from the attic at night. This unnerving phenomenon continued at precisely six monthly intervals. Gibson began to see the white silhouette of a young girl wearing a hooped Victorian skirt, and also sighted a ghostly White Lady standing in front of the drawing room fire.

On 23 May 1968 heavy footsteps were heard crossing the yard. Also at this time the McConnaughey's children saw what they called "a giant bird" in the yard. The aroma of oranges and roses permeated the house, cowbells were heard outside and a bobbing lantern was seen moving from the barn as though an invisible person was carrying it. Then in 1969 Gibson was given a portrait of her grandmother. She had been told that it was a lovely pastel portrait, but when it arrived she found it have been executed in charcoal. A few days after its arrival she heard womens voices in the library where she had hung the picture. Then in February 1970, Cary was sitting in the same room when he was astonished to see colour slowly developing in the portrait, until eventually it became the pastel portrait they had been promised.

A medium was called in to try and clear up the conundrum. She said that Gibson's grandmother, Florence Wright, had died before her portrait was finished and that as such her spirit had become trapped in the picture. Now that it was hung in her granddaughter's home her spirit was free to leave, and it does appear to have done so.

THE PHANTOM HITCH-HIKER OF OKLAHOMA

Winter 1965
Highway 20, nr Claremore, Oklahoma, USA

Mae Doria was driving along Highway 20 when she saw a young lad of about 11 or 12 years of age walking by the side of the road. Mrs Doria gave him a lift and, unlike a lot of phantom hitch-hikers, he was fairly talkative, chatting about playing basketball at school. Mrs Doria was later quite shaken to find out that this young boy had been hitching lifts on Highway 20 since 1936.

THE MIAMI POLTERGEIST

January 1967
Miami, Florida, USA

The poltergeist outbreak here started when objects at a warehouse belonging to a wholesalers called Tropican Arts, began smashing and falling about mysteriously.

On 14 January 1967 the manager, Alvin Laubheim, called the police to the warehouse when he said that a "ghost" was destroying all his goods. The police witnessed many objects falling off the shelves. Psychic investigators, William G Roll and J Gaither Pratt, descended on the scene. They said the catalyst was a 19-year-old clerk called Julio, as the phenomena always occurred when he was around and under stress. Julio denied causing the damage himself, but said that he felt happy when objects broke or fell on the floor.

Carrying out experiments Roll concluded that the phenomena markedly increased when Julio was nearby, and that his own magnetic field was creating a vortex in which the objects "swam". Julio was subjected to psychological tests, and it was found that he was under considerable mental strain. His stepmother had thrown him out of the house just prior to him starting at the warehouse, he disliked his boss, and he continually felt that he was a social outcast. At the end of January Julio was arrested when it was found that he had stolen petty cash from the warehouse. He was sent to prison for six months, and the phenomena at the warehouse ceased. On his release he was reluctantly subjected to further psychological tests, where it was found that he could control his own psychokinesis, similar to the way that some epileptics can induce fits to gain attention.

THE KERN COUNTY HAUNTING
1968
Kern County, California, USA

A desert house was haunted by Mrs Alice Kolitisch, the lady who built the property during the 1920s. When Mr and Mrs Little bought it, Mr Little was disconcerted to find a strange woman wandering around. Then one night, when Frances Little was alone in her bedroom, she watched as a small, thin woman in old-fashioned clothes entered the room. The phantom lady hesitated at the foot of the bed, and then turned and went into the next room. She gave no indication that she had seen Mrs Little. Later, the Littles found a photograph of their ghost and were able to identify her. When they bought the house, Mrs Kolitisch's furniture came with it, and her quiet spirit may have been simply checking that all was still in order.

THE OSCEOLA POLTERGEIST
Autumn 1968
Osceola, South Bend, Indiana, USA

Here two related families were plagued by poltergeist activity, both having household objects thrown around, and rocks hurled at their houses. The stones would rise from the ground by themselves and fly at the windows, causing them to crack.

THE OLIVE HILL POLTERGEIST
November/December 1968
Olive Hill, Kentucky, USA

For two months a boy was followed wherever he went in his home town by poltergeist incidents. It didn't matter which house he was in because furniture would move and crockery would smash, but on one occasion a hazy apparition was seen.

THE PHANTOM SHIP
1969
Block Island Sound, Rhode Island, USA

In 1752 the *Palantine*, an ancient ship even then, set out from Holland crammed with Dutch families eager to start a new life in North America, but there was a potential problem for it was manned by an unscrupulous drunken crew. One evening, around Christmas-time, as they neared the New England coast, the captain had a row with his crew and during the course of it fell, or was pushed, overboard. The crew then robbed the passengers of their valuables and put to sea in a lifeboat. The passengers were rescued by local fishermen, who then looted the ship and set fire to it. Legend has it that after everyone had returned to shore, they could see a terrified woman clinging to the rails of the burning ship. She had hidden below whilst all the plundering had gone on.

Since then, the ship has been said to haunt the Sound at Christmas-time. The locals believed its appearance always warned of stormy weather. A suitably colourful legend one might think, but in 1969 a newspaper *The Westerly Sun* reported that several people had seen "a great red fireball on the ocean". Its burning outline is normally all that is seen, which has led it to being classified as yet another of America's numerous ghost light sightings.

THE PHANTOM CAR OF HIGHWAY 167
20 October 1969
Highway 167, Louisiana, USA

A phantom 1940 black car haunts Highway 167 between Abbeville and Lafayette. It was sighted on this occasion by two men in a car, who noticed that the woman and child wearing old-fashioned 1940s-style clothes in the car behind them, looked rather lost. They debated amongst themselves whether they should stop and ask her if she needed help, but when they looked behind again the car had vanished. They were even more puzzled when the driver behind them said he had seen the black car vanish suddenly in front of him.

THE HAUNTED LIGHTHOUSE
1970s
Point Lookout, Maryland, USA

This haunted lighthouse was extensively investigated throughout the 1970s, and some very interesting phenomena was uncovered. The haunting was brought to the attention of psychic investigators after the resident, Gerald Sword, claimed to hear footsteps, crashes, furniture being moved, doors opening and closing, and various voices. He said he was frequently woken at night by the sound of chattering near the yard gate, but whenever he tried to follow it, the sound always moved on. The investigators set a tape recorder running inside the lighthouse, and when it was played back it revealed a female voice saying "let us not take any objections to what they are doing". A man was heard singing. A female voice was heard shouting "vaccine!" and another man said "fire if they get too close to you", "help me", and "bad shape".

The site around where the lighthouse now stands was used as a hospital during the American Civil War, and many of the noises and comments heard would fit in with that scenario.

THE HAUNTED CINEMA
Early 1970s/mid-1980s
Harvard Exit Theatre, Seattle, Washington, USA

The cinema is based in a turn-of-the-century building, and was created in 1968. During the early 1970s cinema manager, Janet Wainwright, reported seeing the apparition of a woman in Edwardian costume. She also said that she often arrived for work in the morning to find a fire in the grate in a room on the third floor, and chairs grouped in a semi-circle around it. A projectionist reported hearing a woman sobbing on the third floor as well. In 1982 Alan Blangy took over from Janet and was soon to experience phenomena of his own. One night as he was locking up he saw somebody walk out of the fire exit in the third floor auditorium. He ran to the door expecting to see an intruder. It was with great difficulty that he managed to get the door open, but the fire escape was empty and he had heard no footsteps clanging on the stairs. Blangy was considerably shaken by this incident, and he refused to work on his own on the third floor from then on.

In 1985 a group of ghost-hunters left a tape recorder running on the third floor. They claimed to pick up ghostly voices on the tape, but these were highly dubious, as was their claim of seeing a ball of misty light in the auditorium. In 1987 film-maker Karl Krogstad rented part of the theatre to store equipment in. He often reported that boxes were turned over for no reason. Blangy was convinced that the theatre was haunted by Washington's first lady mayor, Bertha K Landes, who had served from 1926 to 1928, and had died in 1943.

Blangy was informed by other members of staff that the fires and re-arranged chairs seen by Janet Wainwright had been practical jokes carried out by them, after she had made a great fuss about seeing the female ghost. In the late 1980s a museum was opened on the other side of Seattle with an exhibition devoted to Bertha K Landes. From then on the haunting at the theatre ceased, and Blangy firmly believes that Bertha has relocated to the museum, although the museum denies experiencing any paranormal phenomena.

THE CLEVELAND POLTERGEIST
July 1970
Cleveland, South Carolina, USA

A family from Cleveland unexpectedly descended on their in-laws, who were living in Springfield, in the hope that they would leave their tiresome poltergeist at home. Wrong, because it followed them, making a nuisance of itself during the visit by pounding on walls and moving objects.

THE POMFRET HAUNTING
1971
Pomfret, Connecticut, USA

Ghostly laughter and other sounds of daily life were heard frequently at an abandoned settlement here. Psychic investigators visited the site and took several photographs, which showed a series of blurred faces and indistinguishable streaks.

THE TRAVELLING POLTERGEIST
1971
Wayne, New Jersey, USA

A family moved from Brooklyn to escape their own poltergeist, only to find that it had followed them to their new home at Wayne and the usual performance of footsteps, knockings and flying objects continued as before.

THE GUARDIAN OF THE PEACH TREES
1971/76
El Paso, Texas, USA

Lila Rosario, 60, was very proud of the two dwarf peach trees that stood on her patio. Larry, a ten-year-old local boy, liked to tease the old lady by pretending to pinch the peaches, and she would react by chasing him down the street. A game that they both equally enjoyed. In 1971 Lila asked Larry to take care of the trees whilst she went to her father's funeral in Utah. Lila died of a heart attack whilst in Salt Lake City, and from then on her ghost gently chided Larry when he tended the trees, in the same way she had done in life. Lila's ghost kept up this little act for five years.

THE HAUNTING OF LONDON BRIDGE
1971
Lake Havasu City, Arizona, USA

A very whimsical 'haunting' this. London Bridge was dismantled stone by stone and shipped to America, where it was re-erected as a tourist attraction next to the 'English Village', a reçonstruction of what the Americans think an English village looks like, complete with London taxi-cabs. Legend has it that since then, the bridge has been haunted by ghosts in Victorian costume, all taking a stroll along the bridge. I suppose ghosts could be counted as part of a typical English scene as well. I think this tale should be taken with a shovel-load of salt, but some may be reminded of the popular old black and while film, *The Ghost Goes West*.

THE PITTSBURGH POLTERGEIST
July 1971/April 1972
Pittsburgh, Pennsylvania, USA

An eventful poltergeist outbreak this one. As well as the usual performance of objects and furniture being moved, there were also bursts of childlike laughter, and misty and shadowy figures seen.

THE APRIL GHOST
1972 and 1980
Oak Bay Golf Course, Victoria, British Columbia, Canada

The April Ghost is so named because she has a habit of appearing regularly from the middle of March and throughout the month of April. She is said to be the ghost of Doris Gravlin who was strangled by her husband, Victor, in 1936, and dumped in one of the sand-traps on the golf course. Doris now appears, normally as a phantom in a white dress, to single people and courting couples. As her own marriage ended in such a dreadful way she now takes it upon herself to warn others of the prospective horrors of matrimony. Those who have seen her have found her pretty terrifying. There was a sighting of her by a couple on 12 March 1972, and a group of teenagers were scared witless by her in 1980.

THE HAUNTED UNIVERSITY
1972
Nebraska Weslyan University, Lincoln, Nebraska, USA

A psychic investigator was called to the university to investigate a haunting that was taking place there. The researcher heard ghostly footsteps whilst on his vigil and felt a wave of intense energy. Eventually it all became too much for him and he fled the building. But it was the feeling of hyper-energy and not the footsteps that terrified him the most he said.

A GHOST CALLED LUCAS
1972/1982
Thomasville, North Carolina, USA

A furniture factory is our next port-of-call for haunted sites. Some workers at a factory here frequently saw a tall ghostly figure of a man, but with blurred features, over a 10-year-period. One imaginative witness claimed to have seen him no less than 50 times. The phantom was a fairly mundane chap, wearing a check work-shirt and khaki trousers, and never spoke to anyone. The workers said he never did any harm and as such accepted him in their midst, nicknaming him "Lucas".

THE HAUNTED FIRE STATION
1972/82
Virginia Beach Fire Station, Virginia, USA

For ten years this fire station was haunted by a very noisy poltergeist. Its activities consisted of slamming the doors, ringing the bells and letting off the sirens. There was also the sound of mysterious clangs, which didn't appear to have any known origin. A very old ghostly fire engine on its way to an emergency perhaps?

THE CHRISTMAS QUILT
1972
Poy Sippi, Wisconsin, USA

When Dora Monroe and her family moved into their new home they discovered an old quilt in a box and, without thinking any more about it, put the quilt on Florence Monroe's bed. Soon after Florence was woken in the night by an invisible presence pulling the quilt from her, and growling "give me back my Christmas quilt!".

THE HAUNTING OF HALCYON HOUSE

1972

Halcyon House, Georgetown, Washington DC, USA

The house was built 200 years ago by Benjamin Stoddert, Secretary of the US Navy. Stoddert had a run of bad luck business-wise, and died penniless in 1813. Since then the house seems to have been unlucky for most of its residents. During the Civil War an underground tunnel was built under the house as part of an underground railway for runaway slaves. Legend has it that some of the slaves died down there and the house has been haunted ever since by their cries and moans. During the 1930s the house was bought by a rather eccentric man who had the belief that if he kept adding onto the house he would never die. As such staircases were erected which led nowhere, and doors opened onto walls. He also refused to have electricity installed.

All his work came to nothing though, for he died in 1938. After his death the haunting increased. Doors and windows opened of their own accord and strange noises were heard coming from the attic. Guests reported waking up to find themselves floating above their beds and an apparition of Benjamin Stoddert was sighted. A phantom woman was also seen in the mid-1970s. In 1972 a couple claimed that they had woken up to find they had been turned round in their bed.

THE BRIDGEPORT POLTERGEIST

Early 1972/75

Bridgeport, Connecticut, USA

A ten-year-old girl called Marcy was at the centre of a poltergeist outbreak here. There were loud banging noises from within the walls, furniture was tipped over and crockery smashed. When the police swooped on young Marcy and accused her of instigating everything they were openly ridiculed.

THE SAN FERNANDO POLTERGEIST

Winter 1972/73

San Fernando, California, USA

A house suffered extensive poltergeist activity here, occasionally involving the radio being interfered with, footsteps heard and sometimes strange apparitions seen.

THE EAST HARTFORD POLTERGEIST

Early 1973/March 1974

East Hartford, Connecticut, USA

An apartment here was said to play host to a poltergeist, whose catalyst was a rag-doll, of all things. It was widely believed that it was possessed by the spirit of a dead girl. When the young lad living in the apartment, Anthony Rossi, frustratingly shouted at it "you're nothing but a toy!" he was immediately seized with a burning sensation in his chest. It was found later that seven bleeding claw-marks were slashed across his body.

THE MITCHELL FLAT GHOST LIGHTS
19 March 1973
Mitchell Flat, nr Marfa, Texas, USA

Ghost lights are a prolific phenomenon in the United States. Sightings of these luminous balls of light form a chain across the country from East to West. They have an affinity with railway tracks and streams, although many have been sighted in the mountains and deserts as well. The spook lights at Joplin, Missouri, have become a source of valuable income to one resident, who charges eager witnesses 25 cents to look through a telescope on the viewing platform erected behind his hut, now turned into a souvenir shop and re-named 'Spookers' Shanty'! A prize winning photograph was taken of one of the lights which appeared at the end of a remote tree-lined road, although to me it looks like somebody approaching on a bicycle!

Robert Ellison first sighted the ghost lights over Mitchell Flat in 1883. They have been seen frequently since then, including on this occasion by two geologists at 10 o'clock at night. Apparently they can usually be seen from Highway 90.

THE PHANTOM ALPINE HOTEL
June 1974
Mount Lowe, California, USA

Bo Linus Orsjo was walking on Mount Lowe when he came across a large green hotel. It was all very peaceful and there didn't seem to be any guests on the premises, only a maid in the hallway sweeping the staircase. Mr Orsjo shrugged and walked on. When he returned to the area two years later, he decided to see if he could find the strange building again, but when he returned to the site he found only its ruins with fully-grown trees growing amongst them. Mr Orsjo was puzzled that a place would have deteriorated so quickly in such a short space of time, until he came across a picture of it in a book. The hotel have been built many years before, as part of a planned Alpine village complex, but had been forced to close after several fires had broken out ... in 1937, some 35 years before his first sighting of the building.

THE AMITYVILLE HORROR
mid-1970s
112 Ocean Avenue, Amityville, New York, USA

On 13 November 1974 Ronald deFeo walked around his house in the middle of the night and shot dead his entire family as they lay sleeping. Just over a year later on 18 December 1975 George and Kathy Lutz moved into deFeo's old house with their three children, and claimed to endure a terrifying haunting. The large Dutch colonial house was a snip at only 80,000 dollars, because no one wanted to live in a building that had such a horrific recent past. According to the bestselling book by Jay Anson which detailed the haunting, the Lutzes endured black slime bubbling out of their toilets, hooded spectres, an attack of killer bees, cold spots, the sound of an invisible brass band in the living-room, doors slamming, green slime coming out of the walls, their daughter talking to an invisible friend (hardly an unusual occurrence where children are concerned), and the imprints of cloven hooves found in the grounds outside! George grew a beard and claimed that he began to take on the appearance of Ronald deFeo. He stopped going to work and his business suffered. Father Ralph Pecararo said he heard a voice telling him to get out when he sprinkled the house with holy water. A small room was found beneath the stairs, painted entirely in blood red, but no use for the room was ever discovered. On 14 January 1976 the Lutzes fled the house in the middle of the night, never to return.

A string of turgid films followed. The first, which was about the Lutzes experiences, was incredibly dire and downright dull, and seemed to claim that in Amityville a violent thunderstorm occurred every night! Both the book and the film were quite shameless in the lies they told. Anson had claimed that the manuscript was jinxed and attributed everything that happened, including driving his car into a hole, as "The Curse of The Manuscript". On the set of the film James Brolin, who played George Lutz, claimed to be equally affected, suffering an accident in a lift and a wrenched ankle. The original house, accurately called 'High Hopes', was not used in the film because it was said that no one liked the atmosphere there. Anson, who was prone to ill-health, never actually visited the house he wrote about.

At first sight this whole catalogue of events might be impressive, were it not for the fact that the haunting itself was an outrageous fraud, committed by a mixed-up family who were on their uppers financially. After their dramatic flight from the house the Lutzes went to live in California, where they continued to write books about the haunting, claiming that the 'demons' had followed them there. These experiences were chronicled in the third Amityville film *Amityville: The Final Chapter* (if only!), in which the names of the Lutzes children had been mysteriously changed for no reason, and George Lutz, who worked in a family surveying company, now found himself as an air traffic controller.

Tellingly, the subsequent owners of 'High Hopes', Jim and Barbara Cromarty, said that the house isn't haunted at all. They successfully sued the Lutzes and Jay Anson, because they had had to suffer inordinately from sensation-seekers since the "haunting" went public. Father Pecararo also sued the Lutzes for invasion of privacy, and distortion of facts. He settled out of court.

The sceptics fell on the Amityville Horror with unrestrained glee. It was fairly easy to tear it to pieces, for instance some of the terrible weather described in Anson's 'factual' book could be denounced simply by checking actual weather reports. The details of Father Pecararo's experiences were found to have been concocted by Anson from taped telephone interviews made many months before, and based solely on the one visit Father Pecararo made to the house. Much more damning though, was the interview Ronald deFeo's lawyer gave on radio in 1979. He said the whole haunting had been cooked up around the Lutzes' kitchen table over several bottles of wine! He sued them for a share in the profits from the book and the film. The Lutzes sued him back, and Kathy took part in a

Psychological Stress Evaluator, which concluded that she believed the events to have actually happened. The Lutzes have consistently refused to face their critics in a televised confrontation though.

Judge Jack Weinstein, who presided over one of the many libel cases concerned with the Amityville Farce said that "the evidence shows fairly clearly that the Lutzes during this entire period were considering and acting with the thought of having a book published". Dr Stephen Kaplan, the director of the Parapsychology Institute of America, studied the case for months and interviewed many of the people involved. He should have the final say on this whole sordid mess. "We found no evidence to support any claim of a 'haunted house'. What we did find is a couple who had purchased a house that they economically could not afford. It is our professional opinion that the story of its haunting is mostly fiction". It happens.

THE HAUNTING OF MCLOUGHLIN HOUSE

mid-1970s/late 1980s

McLoughlin House, Oregon City, Oregon, USA

This house is named after its first owner, Dr John D McLoughlin (1784-1857), a pioneer and the founder of Oregon City. No phenomena was reported in the house whatsoever until the mid-1970s when Nancy Wilson took over as curator of the house, now a museum. It has to be said that Nancy had no interest in ghosts or the supernatural until inexplicable things began happening on a regular basis, usually at the rate of once a week, and usually when the house was closed to the public. One day when working alone upstairs, she felt a firm tap on her shoulder but on looking round found no one was there. However, soon afterwards both Nancy and other members of staff began to see a large apparition (McLoughlin was 6ft 5in in height) walking up the stairs and into McLoughlin's old bedroom.

The sound of heavy boots could also be heard, and the aroma of fresh ground coffee detected. Every year on 3 September, the anniversary of McLoughlin's death, his portrait is said to emit a strange and eerie glow, and staff have arrived at the house in the morning to find a child's bed looking as though it has been slept in. Nancy claims to have heard a woman's voice crying pathetically for help. The activity peaked in 1981 when the curator arranged an exhibition of pioneering clothing at the house. McLoughlin's ghost has continued to make himself felt ever since, but the staff insist they do not feel threatened by him. Nancy has since researched her family history and has found a link between her ancestors and McLoughlin.

At one time a Mrs Wells, a distant ancestor of the curator, borrowed 43 dollars from McLoughlin, but she died before she could pay him back. Nancy believes McLoughlin is showing approval of her work in the house, as though to say that old debts are settled at last.

THE AYERSVILLE WATER SPOOK

5/10 July 1975

Ayersville, Ohio, USA

For a week there were inexplicable spurts of water inside a house here. The water would appear anywhere, on floors, on top of the piano and even inside drawers, yet the ceilings and walls would remain completely dry. A baffled plumber said that he could find no leak to account for the mystery.

THE GHOST IN TWEEDS

Autumn 1976

Grand Rapids, Michigan, USA

An old mansion here was haunted by the sound of footsteps and the scent of roses. On one occasion the ghost of an old man wearing brown tweeds was seen leaning against the mantlepiece. He tipped his hat politely and then walked away through a closed door.

THE PEARISBURG POLTERGEIST

December 1976

Pearisburg, Virginia, USA

Mrs Beulah Wilson's nine-year-old foster child was the catalyst at the heart of this poltergeist outbreak. It consisted of the usual chaotic mayhem of furniture being moved and crockery smashed.

RESURRECTION MARY
December 1977
Resurrection Cemetery, Archer Avenue, Justice, Chicago, Illinois, USA

Archer Avenue is haunted by a female phantom hitch-hiker nicknamed 'Resurrection Mary', because she is buried in Resurrection Cemetery in the same area. She is identifiable from her attractive 1920s costume, her blonde hair and blue eyes and she always asks to be dropped off at the cemetery! In December 1977 a motorist saw her peering through the iron bars of the cemetery gates. The story is that she was a Polish girl who had a row with her boyfriend and was knocked down by a car on her way home from a dance in 1934. She has been witnessed fairly regularly since then. In 1939 she terrified one driver by jumping on the running-board of his car.

Rumour has it that she also puts in an appearance at the old ballroom where she spent her last evening. In Mary's day it was O'Henry Ballroom, nowadays it is called the Willowbrook Ballroom. There she is said to mingle with the other dancers. Men who have unwittingly partnered her have said that her skin is icy cold and she seemed rather aloof. Sightings of her have increased since the mid-1970s when the cemetery was renovated, which possibly disturbed her ghost even more. The cemetery itself is also haunted by ghostly monks who were seen late in 1977 by police officers. The ghosts vanished as the law approached.

THE HAUNTING OF HAM HOUSE
1978
Ham House, Dubuque, Iowa, USA

The house was built in 1857 by wealthy businessman Mathias Ham, who constructed it out of limestone he had bought at a knockdown price from a federal inspector. The end product was a luxurious Gothic mansion. The Hams were respected in local society, and one of Mathias's little hobbies was to retire to his den on the third floor and watch the boats on the river. On one occasion he witnessed pirates plying their trade and reported them to the appropriate authorities. The pirates vowed revenge. Ham's wife died in 1874 and he followed her in 1889, leaving their daughter Sarah alone in the house. One night Sarah heard a prowler and fearing it was the pirates coming back for their revenge, she picked up a gun and fired through a door.

The intruder was shot and staggered out of the house. In the morning the body of a pirate was found on the riverbank. Sarah escaped judicial punishment and died in 1911. The murder story is shaky though, as none of the doors in the house, all original, show any sign of having patched bullet holes in them. Nonetheless, many swear that the house is definitely haunted. In 1964 the house was turned into a museum and since then the employees there have reported strange phenomena. A window in an upstairs hall is found persistently open every morning and a light goes on and off by itself in the hallway. A cold spot has been detected by the stairs leading to Mathias's den and organ music was once heard coming out of a fuse box!

An employee stayed a night in the house in 1978. He woke at 3 AM to hear women's voices in the yard, and footsteps and shuffling noises.

THE LEESBURG POLTERGEIST
January 1978/79
Leesburg, Florida, USA

We have a very curious poltergeist case with this one. It all began when mysterious voices interrupted a telephone conversation at the house in question, but this was no mere crossed line. It heralded a year-long series of disturbing paranormal phenomena. There was the usual movement of furniture and household objects, but even more disconcerting were the strange voices that came out of the walls, and even out of the mouth of the ten-year-old daughter. The house was entirely occupied by women; the grandmother, mother, and two daughters, the youngest of whom was six. The strange voices were far from welcome as they often used rather colourful language and made abusive threats.

The strangest phenomenon of all was when the voices would interrupt phone calls and proceed to give lengthy descriptions of the person on the other end of the line!

THE HAZLET STONE SHOWER
June 1978
Elm Avenue, Hazlet, New Jersey, USA

A house was the target of several virulent stone showers. Large rocks and bits of concrete rained down, causing windows to be broken and cars to be damaged. The police grew so frustrated by the phenomenon that they arrested a young lad for throwing a pebble at his garage doors.

THE LITTLE BOY IN WHITE
1979/81
Grant, New England, USA

A small boy dressed in white haunted the home of an unnamed family here. On 9 March 1981 the wife of the owner was sitting at home alone with the children, as her husband was working on night shift at a local factory. In the early hours of the morning she awoke to see a small boy, dressed in white, standing outside her bedroom door. It couldn't have been her own son, because he was 15, and this child looked no older than eight. She watched him pacing the hallway for some considerable time. A few days later, on 20 March, she saw him again. This time he spoke to her, asking pathetically "Where do all the lonely people go?" and "Where do I belong?"

Three days later her husband saw the little boy in their bedroom, where the child told him that lies had been told and it was time for the truth. Their daughter, who was 11, was frightened by seeing the little lad and dived under her bedclothes. It was commonly believed to be the owner's uncle, who had died when a child and had been buried in his white communion suit. The house had been built around the time of his birth. The lies he referred to could have related to his twin brother, who was blamed for taking something from the house. On one occasion the owner was talking to his father on the phone, and every time he mentioned his uncle, the line went dead.

When they were advised by someone at their Catholic church to ignore the boy, poltergeist phenomena broke out, with a telephone being flung across the room and a closet door slammed. Even more disturbing was the sound of crying in the house which tended to precede some ill-luck for the family. In May 1979 the owner's wife heard it just prior to her daughter's operation. Another spectre at this psychically-overcrowded site, was that of a grotesque hunched figure who mouthed obscenities. It was believed to be the owner's grandmother, who resented his wife and had been opposed to their marriage.

Lights and the water supply were turned on and off at the house, and bedclothes and religious knick-knacks were moved. An exorcism seemed to calm the more aggressive nature of the phenomena. William Ross, a director of the Psychical Research Foundation, believed the phenomena was brought on by stresses within the family.

THE GHOST OF EDITH WHARTON
1979
The Mount, Lenox, Massachusetts, USA

American author Edith Wharton built The Mount at the turn of the 20th century. It was a pleasant neo-Georgian mansion where she liked to work and entertain friends. In 1912 Edith sold it and for a while the house was used as a girl's school. In 1978 it was taken over by 'Shakespeare and Company', a troupe of actors that live and perform in the house. The actors have reported considerable phenomena here, from the sounds of girlish laughter, thought to belong to the time when the house was a school, to an apparition of Edith Wharton sighted on the second floor, and seen walking up and down the terrace. There is also the less pleasant phantom of a hooded figure who presses people down as they lie in bed.

In 1979 Andrea Haring, an actress and voice teacher, who was sleeping in Edith's old study, suddenly woke at 4 AM , to find the room had gone icy cold and saw three figures, and a desk and divan that had appeared out of nowhere. She said the furniture and the people seemed quite real. One of the phantoms, Edith, was sitting at her desk writing and talking to two men, one of whom Andrea recognised as Edith's husband Edward. Although they all seemed to be conversing normally, Andrea couldn't hear what was being said, but suddenly the ghosts turned to her and seemed to acknowledge her presence (very unusual!).

Andrea left the room, and when she returned it was empty of ghosts and their furniture. The second man Andrea saw, is thought to be Edith's secretary, who many speculate was also her lover.

THE WOODHAVEN BOOM
April 1979
Woodhaven, Michigan, USA

A house was plagued by the sound of a loud 'boom' every half-an-hour. The noise was so loud and strong that it vibrated the floor. Such mundane matters as gas leaks, sewer gas and the plumbing were all successfully ruled out as the cause.

NOISES FROM THE PAST
Early 1980s
Fairley Lampman Building, Cripple Creek, Colorado, USA

Echoes of a bygone age were recorded here. Voices and footsteps were heard, as well as dancing in the ballroom, and the sound of a typewriter clicking. The apparition of a young woman was sighted and heady perfume detected in one of the rooms.

THE PHANTOM COOK
Early 1980s
Lampasas, Texas, USA

The aromatic smell of frying liver and onions haunted an old house here every Friday night during the early 1980s. The Bradleys, whose home it was, concluded that the phantom cook was Adelaide Higdon, a previous owner. There was also the recurring sound of a door slamming in the place where there used to be a doorway. The haunting was accepted by the family, and Mrs Bradley even used to address the invisible ghost until it started tossing plates about. Mrs Bradley decided to ignore it, a feeling that was strengthened when she heard about how mean Adelaide Higdon had been during her lifetime. Soon after the ostracism by the Bradleys, the aromatic cooking smells perpetrated, one assumes by Adelaide's ghost, ceased.

PARTIAL SHC
19 June 1980
Toronto, Ontario, Canada

Here was a rare example of a mild attack of, or what might have been, Spontaneous Human Combustion. But this victim lived to tell the tale! A 31-year-old woman went to bed and after four hours sleep woke up to find that she had second and third degree burns on her thighs and abdomen, although her nightclothes and bedlinen were unsinged.

THE LEE POLTERGEIST
1981
Lee, Massachusetts, USA

A poltergeist produced a devastating exhibition of hate at the home of a Catholic family here. It decapitated religious statues, threw a crucifix downstairs and rammed a butcher's knife into the kitchen table. Vague apparitions were also sighted during the outbreak. It's probable that someone in the family was going through a crisis of conscience about their faith and this was manifesting itself in this severe poltergeist phenomenon.

THE BAKERSFIELD HAUNTING
30 November 1981/25 January 1982
Bakersfield, California, USA

A very strange and rather muddled haunting this, like two cases clumsily stitched together. On 30 November 1981 Mrs Frances Freeborn moved into a house that had remained more or less unoccupied since the death of the previous owner, an unnamed widow, in 1976. Mrs Freeborn sensed that the lady did not approve of the changes she was making to the house, and pictures were found moved to lower positions on the walls (the previous owner had been a very short woman). All this was very harmless, and Mrs Freeborn never felt in any danger until 25 January 1982. She had been planning to decorate the main bedroom, but suddenly felt as though she was being watched.

After going to bed for the night she heard a disturbing noise as though the kitchen was being smashed up and terrified out of her wits, she tried to leave the house, but encountered a "wall of pressure" in the hallway trying to impede her exit. She claimed to have seen three entities, one of whom was a little boy, before managing to flee the house in her nightie. This peculiar and controversial haunted house has since been exorcised.

THE HAUNTED COTTAGE
1982
Las Vegas, Nebraska, USA

Hilary Spence visited her aunt in Greater Manchester, England, and took a shine to a small pottery container, known as a 'cottage', in her house. Aunt Jean willingly gave it to her and Hilary returned home to Las Vegas with it. Soon after she noticed a shadow lurking near her bathroom door, and saw a ghostly male figure walking through her house. Her daughter Billie began to remark on how cold the bungalow felt, and when she commented on how much she liked the pottery container, Hilary gave it to her. Billie then started to see the shadow in her own home. She tried various ways of exorcising the 'cottage' until one day she simply emptied it completely of all its contents. The haunting then ceased.

A whimsical theory is that the 'cottage' was the home of the apparition, and it didn't have room to live there whilst it was full of odds-and-ends.

THE GHOSTLY GENEALOGIST
1982, 1983 and 1985
New Hanover County Library, Wilmington, North Carolina, USA

A deceased lady genealogist haunts the library. Books were often heard moving on the shelves, seemingly of their own accord. Nobody knew who she could be, until one day a man visited the library, saw the ghost and recognised her as an old colleague. He called out her name, and she then made a very untypical ghostly movement by looking straight at him and fleeing, and then disappeared behind the stacks.

THE CROSBY POLTERGEIST
1982/87
Crosby, Texas, USA

Shades of the movie *Poltergeist* in this case. A house was built over an old graveyard here, and it was thence plagued with poltergeist activity, and a neighbour claimed to see ghosts in one of the bedrooms.

THE HAUNTED CEMETERY
1982
Bachelor's Grove Cemetery, Chicago, Illinois, USA

The haunted hotspot in Chicago it would seem. Although the cemetery has been disused since 1965, it hasn't stopped the numerous legends that have sprung up around it. The cemetery is now in a sorry state, overgrown and frequently inflicted with vandals and satanists, as evidence of animal sacrifices and mutilated graves have been found there (we have a similar example in Britain with the cemetery at St Mary's Church, Clophill in Bedfordshire). Many of the ghost stories connected with this place belong firmly in the realm of local entertainment, and their cousins can be found the world over.

Apparitions of hooded spectres have been sighted,

plus a crying woman carrying a baby, and a phantom farmhouse has been appearing at random since the 1950s, even though no farmhouse has ever existed in the area. More substantial are the ghost lights that are said to haunt the locality. Other reports are of inexplicable cold spots and the sensation of being watched by unseen eyes. In 1982 Dale Kaczmarek, President of the Ghost Research Society, took a medium to the cemetery and she reported that there were various ghosts there, who were frustrated because they couldn't leave the confines of the cemetery. Attempts were made to photograph the frustrated spirits with an infra-red camera, but the first half of the roll was found to be mysteriously wiped out, although photographs taken elsewhere were unharmed.

THE WHARNCLIFFE FIRE SPOOK

Summer 1983

Wharncliffe, West Virginia, USA

This small town was plagued by outbreaks of fire during the summer of 1983. Nothing was safe from the fire spook. Houses were reduced to smoking ruins, flames shot out of disused electrical sockets, clothing in a trunk smouldered, and even wasps were found with burnt wings. This case bears strong resemblences to the San Gottardo one in Italy. Was excessive electricity being pumped into Wharncliffe as well perhaps?

THE ARIZONA STONE SHOWERS
Autumn 1983
The Arizona Desert, USA

The home of the Berkbigler family, a remote house here in the desert, was invaded by a torrent of stone showers. For three months it was bombarded daily with rocks, and in all 79 episodes of such a phenomenon were recorded. Many of the stones dented the cars outside, causing damage of up to 7000 dollars. The throwing was so regular that it was confined to between the hours of 5.30 and 7.00 in the evening, and was sometimes accompanied by a strange knocking on the doors and windows. On 4 December some reporters visited the Berkbiglers and found themselves trapped in the house for two hours by a particularly vicious bombardment.

Then on 7 December, the phenomenon ceased abruptly never to start again. The Berkbiglers had three children, aged 20, 19 and 15, any of whom of course could have been the poltergeist's catalyst.

THE OLD EMPTY HOUSE
Spring 1984
Pores Knob, Wilkes County, North Carolina, USA

Two young men camped out for the night in an abandoned house in Pores Knob, a remote area in Wilkes County. Every window of the house was found to be broken but the men set up camp in one of the ground floor rooms. They were woken a short while later by the sound of glass being picked up and dropped inside the house, accompanied by scratching noises and the doorknob turning. They found out the next day that, like many remote and abandoned houses, the house was rumoured to be haunted.

THE COLONIE BOOM
August/September 1984
Colonie, New York, USA

Sounds like artillery shells exploding were heard at a house here. The noises were usually heard at night, and were so loud they caused vibrations in the ground. All the usual possibilities, such as gas, sewers, water and electric lines were positively ruled out.

THE SMURL HAUNTING
1985/87
West Pittston, Pennsylvania, USA

Another haunting that has caused considerable controversy in America which also has possibilities of being a new Amityville. The Smurl family had lived in a duplex here since 1973, with John and Mary Smurl living in the right half, and their son Jack, his wife Janet and their two daughters, Dawn and Heather, in the other half. They all stress that they were a happy, contented group, being devout Catholics, and Jack and Janet were quite happy to live with Jack's parents. But they had been plagued by strange events in the duplex ever since they moved in. TV sets had burst into flames, pipes leaked and paintwork was scratched, toilets were flushed, footsteps were heard on the stairs and the radio blared out even when it was unplugged. Strange smells were also detected.

Twin daughters, Shannon and Carin, were born in 1977 and the Smurls were by now getting a bit tired of the inexplicable disturbances. Things were to get far worse though. In 1985 all the rooms mysteriously became icy cold. Obscene voices were heard when no one was talking,and Janet heard her name being called in the basement. Then in February, Janet saw a huge black apparition with no face in the kitchen! It walked through the wall and Mary saw it on the other side. From then on the family knew little peace. On the night Heather was to be confirmed, Jack was levitated into the air and on another occasion Janet was pulled out of bed whilst making love to her husband, and Jack nearly gagged when he smelt foul odours.

The family dog was lifted into the air and physically attacked by an unseen force. Little Shannon was tossed out of bed, and the sound of hissing snakes was heard. Neighbours reported hearing screaming from the house when the entire family was out. Reluctantly, in January 1986, the Smurls called in psychic researchers, Ed and Lorraine Warren. The Warrens questioned the Smurls exhaustively about their religious beliefs and announced that the duplex was haunted by no less than four 'demons'. There was no bad feeling amongst the family, so the Warrens concluded that the 'creatures' were being activated by the daughters' approaching puberty. The Warrens arranged a prayer session to try and coax at least one of the demons into the open.

They were interrupted by a voice growling "You filthy bastard. Get out of this house". The TV set emitted an eerie glow, and a mirror shook. After that Janet was punched and slapped. Jack then saw the ghosts of two women dressed in Colonial clothing and things began to get very dramatic indeed. Jack claimed to be sexually assaulted by a hideous succubus posing as a grotesque old woman. Grunting noises like pigs were heard throughout the house, and although the family tried to get help from the Catholic Church, they proved to be very non-committal. However, Father Robert F McKenna performed an exorcism, which only made things worse. The 'demons' followed Jack to work,and accompanied the family when they went camping. The Smurls knew that moving wasn't the answer, for the ghosts would probably just follow.

After the family had appeared anonymously on local television, the 'demon' went mad with rage. It levitated Janet into the air and hurled her against the wall, and Jack saw a monstrous creature resembling a pig on two legs. In August 1986 the family's story was reported in the press. Immediately their house became a tourist attraction, which confirmed many sceptical neighbours beliefs that the family was hoping to benefit from a book contract. The Amityville spectre still loomed large it would seem. The Smurls didn't help their cause by rebuffing the advances of scientific and psychic investigators, claiming that they preferred to work with the Church and the very dubious Warren couple.

CSICOP, the organisation which sets out to denounce paranormal phenomena, concluded that the haunting was due to an abandoned mine shaft nearby which could cause the strange noises, a broken sewer pipe which could generate the foul smells, and pranks by teenagers. They also concluded that Jack had fantasised that he was being raped by a ghost. It was also pointed out, damningly, that although Janet said she had reported their troubles to the police, the police had no record of her getting in touch with them. Ed Warren claimed to have videotapes of the noises heard in the house and a dark shape moving about. When asked by CSICOP to produce them, he said they were in the possession of the Church. The Church promptly denied having them.

He also refused the request of some journalists who wanted to spend a night in the house. It seemed very much as though Ed Warren had taken over the entire case. Press coverage finally forced the Church to take action, and they graciously offered to look into the haunting and perform a genuine exorcism. The Smurls moved away in 1988, and after a final exorcism they seem to have been left alone by their 'demons'. A book and a film, both called *The Haunted,* have since followed. No doubt this case, like the Amityville Horror, will degenerate into the usual mess of endless lawsuits as the years go on.

PHANTOM VOICES ON TAPE
Autumn 1986
Calvert County, Maryland, USA

A psychic investigator visited a haunted house here and recorded some intriguing ghostly voices on tape. "I'm up here", "I can help you", "I like you", "they're going to kill me", "I killed for you" and "it's near his vault" were some of the comments being mysteriously aired from beyond the grave.

ERNIE'S DOMAIN
May 1987
New London Ledge Lighthouse, nr New London, Connecticut, USA

This lighthouse, which was established in 1910, is believed to be haunted by the ghost of a former lighthouse keeper, known to posterity only as 'Ernie'. Legend has it that Ernie threw himself from the top of the lighthouse after he found out that his wife had run off with another man. The story largely belongs in the realm of mythology, as the lighthouse logbook fails to record such a dramatic event anywhere in its history. Nonetheless lighthouse keepers over the years have consistently heard footsteps going up the stairs, reported rooms going cold for no reason, doors closing, and chairs moving by themselves. If there is no ghost of Ernie, then the lighthouse haunting is a very good example of how strongly a person's surroundings can affect them.

Being a lighthouse keeper was the loneliest job in the world. Men were frequently left at very remote locations for great lengths of time and it would not be surprising if the eerie atmosphere of the isolated New London Ledge Lighthouse, combined with the story of the non-existent Ernie, induced paranormal phenomena around some lighthouse keepers. The whole atmosphere of the lighthouse is summed up in the final log-book entry, made when the Light went fully automatic on 1 May 1987. "Rock of slow torture. Ernie's domain. Hell on Earth - may New London Ledge's light shine forever because I'm through. I will watch it from afar while drinking a brew".

THE BLOOD SPOOK OF ATLANTA
September 1987
Atlanta, Georgia, USA

Human blood (identified by experts as type 'O') seeped in profusion from the floors at the home of an elderly couple. Mr and Mrs William Winston, aged 79 and 71 respectively, had no idea why they should suddenly be 'honoured' with such a bloodbath. On one occasion Mrs Winston stepped out of the bath to find the bathroom floor saturated with blood. The police were called and arrived to find the substance dripping from the walls and floors in five separate rooms. This particular case is inexplicable in all respects, especially as the inhabitants of the house were of such an advanced age. Everyone involved in the case expressed themselves to be completely baffled.

THE GHOST OF EAST 62ND STREET
October 1987
East 62nd Street, New York City, USA

A woman arrived early at her new office job to be greeted by a man whom she mistook for the porter, and who let her into the locked building. But later when she described him to her colleagues, she was told he was really Angelo Donghia, an interior designer ... and he was dead.

THE METHODIST CHURCH LIGHT

November 1987

Absaraka, North Dakota, USA

An abandoned and empty Methodist church here was seen to be mysteriously illuminated by a light in the shape of a cross. It was seen one night by boys exploring the building. A number of other witnesses flocked to the site and confirmed the boys' story.

THE CLIFTON FIRE SPOOK

began 31 January 1988

Clifton, New Jersey, USA

A fire spook invaded Jerry Siciliano's home. The phenomena seemed to confine itself mostly to the electrical fixtures. Mr Siciliano cut the power off but the spontaneous fires continued. He called in the local fire chief, who admitted to being baffled. In desperation, Jerry threw his hands in the air and moved himself and his family out of the house.

THE VIRGIN MARY IN TEXAS

began February 1988

Lubbock, Texas

Three parishioners of the St John Neumann Roman Catholic Church reported that, whilst they were saying their Rosaries, the Virgin Mary had appeared to them and given them messages of peace and love. Mary said she would return at the Feast of the Assumption in

August. About 20,000 people gathered around the church on that day, and many reported seeing a vision of Mary, as well as the head of Jesus. From then on the people of Lubbock began going to church more regularly, and miracle cures have been said to have taken place.

THE GHOST THAT MADE LEGAL HISTORY

July 1991

Nyack, New York, USA

A haunted house here made legal history. Jeffrey and Patrice Stambousky sued for the return of the 32,500 dollar deposit after they found that it was haunted by a smiling ghost in Revolutionary costume who had a habit of floating in mid-air. The Stambouskys won their case when the jury voted 3:2 that they should have been informed that the house was haunted before they moved in.

THE COMMISSIONER'S SUICIDE
1871
Hoshiarpur, Punjab, India

Mr and Mrs Troward arrived at Hoshiarpur to take up their new duties, but when they moved into their bungalow they were informed that the servants didn't want to stay there, and were advised that they shouldn't stay there either. The Trowards were too tired to listen and insisted on remaining. In the middle of the night Mr Troward was woken by his wife screaming. She said she had seen a man in a grey suit standing by the bed. He had told her "lie still, I shall not hurt you" before firing a gun over her. The following morning the Trowards heard that the previous commissioner, Mr DeCourcy, had shot himself in their bedroom, after reassuring his terrified wife that he wouldn't hurt her.

THE LEGEND OF THE PENANGGAL
1895
Changkat Asah, Malaya

Local legend has it that when a woman dies in childbirth she becomes a hideous spirit known as a 'Penanggal'. At night her head and part of her entrails rise up from the grave, and she flies through the air, sucking the blood out of any man she sees. She must return to her grave before daybreak. An interesting variation on the vampire legend, but in modern eyes the spirit is more commonly associated with ghost lights. Sir George Maxwell lived near a hill called Changkat Asah. The locals wasted no time telling him that the hill was haunted by the 'Penanggal'. Beginda Sutan, a brave man, scorned the legend and decided to camp out on the hill all night but by morning he was found to be completely insane.

Sir George met Beginda himself, and realised that he was indeed deranged, yet he camped out on the hill one night, on the lookout for a tiger that had terrorised an officer. He saw two ghost lights come speeding towards him, each about the size of a human head. Maxwell realised it was a natural phenomenon though, and wasn't afraid. During the night he saw nearly 100 of these lights, dancing around the area, wafted along by the currents of air. He knew that they must have driven Beginda insane, as well they could to any man who had been so culturally conditioned. It was a tragic fact that Beginda had lost his mind because he had seen what were only balls of phosphorous gas.

THE SUMATRAN STONE SHOWER
September 1903
Sumatra, Indonesia

W D Grottendieck, an engineer from Holland, had just returned from a tiring trip through the Sumatran jungle with 50 coollies and collapsed for the night at a new house that had just been erected on bamboo poles. At 1 o'clock in the morning the engineer was woken by stones falling near his head. He turned up his kerosene lamp and noted that the stones seemed to be falling down from the roof, although there was no hole in the thatching. Grottendieck woke up his servant boy in the next room and told him to go outside and check if anyone was there. Whilst the boy did so Grottendieck continued to watch the stones dropping onto the floor of the hut. Grottendieck tried to catch some of the stones, but found them to be very elusive. He claimed many floated away just as he reached out for them.

He climbed the partition to see where the stones could be coming from but found nothing to account for this bizarre phenomenon. In frustration he fired his rifle five times into the air, mainly to try and scare away any pranksters, but the stones kept falling. His servant boy announced that it was all the work of Satan and fled into the jungle. Grottendieck never saw him again, but as soon as the boy left the stone shower ceased. By morning 18 to 24 of the stones still remained on the hut floor. Grottendieck ruled out the possibility of the boy tricking him because whilst he was bending over him and trying to wake him up, he could see the stones continuing to fall through a gap in the partition.

Grottendieck, hitherto a confirmed sceptic on paranormal matters, believed that the stone throwing was being caused by his sister who had died three months before. He believed she was trying to get in touch with him.

THE POONA POLTERGEIST
1927/1930
Poona, India

A guest at a house here kept a diary of the poltergeist phenomena, and some of the things she witnessed were truly extraordinary. Miss Kohn was staying at the home of the Ketkar family. On 28 July 1928 she noted that soon after one of the boys, Damodar, had gone to bed his toys began to move by themselves. His wooden toy box was slammed shut and the lid firmly secured, but the toys kept moving and threw themselves at his bed. The phenomena had been happening since the previous April, and Damodar had refused to sleep under a mosquito net because then the toys had become trapped in the bed with him. Miss Kohn placed a large heavy dictionary on the toy box, but this failed to stop the activity.

One night a jar flew into Miss Kohn's bedroom, it turned out to be a jar that Damodar had taken to school a few days before. On 26 July, Miss Kohn was sitting next to Damodar in her bedroom when a glass button was dropped into a small bowl in which a candle was burning. On another occasion, Damodar was 'teleported' to the car which was shut inside a closed shed and his elder brother also materialised in a doorway, hovering a short way off the floor. Fruit was left out to placate the spirit, and later the family heard 'lip-smacking' noises and the rinds reappeared later bearing toothmarks. Less pleasant were the occasions when Damodar was bitten and slapped, his baby sister had her bib knotted so tightly that she nearly choked to death, and his parents were scratched, pinched and smeared with saliva.

On 23 May 1928, which was Damodar's ninth birthday, he was pelted with stones. Miss Kohn kept a close watch on him and when she checked his pockets, she found them full of stones. In view of all the other incredible phenomena that had taken place, she didn't believe he was guilty of hoaxing though, and concluded that the poltergeist had a bizarre sense of humour. That has frequently been found to be the case!

THE GUARDIAN OF THE TREASURE
1928
Arakan, Burma

One evening Maurice Collis was working late when he felt the entire building shake around him. He then saw a woman in white standing on the steps, but she passed out of sight. The locals believed her to be a female spirit bound to the earth to guard the 'old king's treasure'. She would have been buried alive to make sure she stayed on the earth. When he asked why the house had shaken so much, they said it was because she wanted to attract his attention. She certainly did that.

TONG TANGJIANG - FIRESTARTER
30 April 1990
Hunan Province, China

A four year old boy, Tong Tangjiang, was able it seems to produce smoke from his trousers, right hand, armpits and genitals. For two hours he was kept under observation in a hospital in the Hunan Province and whilst there, it was noted that he spontaneously ignited four times. Dr Hsing Peng, who investigated Tong's dilemma, concluded that the boy had a strong electrical current running through his body, which intensified under stress, nervousness or excitement. Tong's fire-starting abilities led him to being ostracised by neighbours and friends who were too scared to get near him.

THE RETURN OF MARIAMMA
Early 1991
Pondicherry, India

An extremely unnerving apparition was scaring the inhabitants of this town during the early months of 1991. The spectre of a woman, described as "having eyes all over her face" was sighted by many witnesses wandering around the village streets. The villagers believed her to be the apparition of their goddess Mariamma, and decorated every building and vehicle in the village with garlands of neem leaves to try and appease her. We have yet to hear if it worked.

THE MIRACLE OF ZARKA
21 April 1991
Zarka, nr Amman, Jordan

Sounds like something from *The Life of Brian* this one. A priest was preparing for communion at a church in Zarka when blood suddenly began to pour from the bread. The worshippers went into a frenzy and daubed their faces with it, whilst a local man who had been bedridden for years suddenly tore off his oxygen mask and sprang out of bed. A miracle was officially declared a few days later.

THE STONE SHOWERS OF TURKEY
Summer 1992
Cataltepe, Kakta Town, Adiyaman, Turkey

For ten days stones fell near the tomb of a Muslim saint near the village of Cataltepe. Villagers believed the saint was punishing them for their bad ways. The showers always occurred between 8 and 10 o'clock in the evening.

THE PHILIPPINO DEMON
January 1993
Quezon City, The Philippines

Joy Balante, 12, and some school chums at Camp Crame Elementary School burnt some wood at the bottom of a tamarind tree. When the flames died down the children claimed to see a gigantic black man with a tail and horns.

Joy was so distressed that she collapsed and was sent home from school. When she regained consciousness she spoke in a man's voice and shouted "There is no God!". Two days later, five of her classmates began talking in different voices and displaying great physical strength. Fifteen others collapsed for no specific reason. All the children were subsequently carted off to a Roman Catholic church and splattered with holy water.

THE WEEPING VIRGIN OF BARINGJAY

11 February 1993

Baringjay, San Antonio, Agoo, La Union, The Philippines

A statue of the Virgin Mary shed tears of blood here on the feast day of Our Lady of Lourdes. Hours later dried blood was still to be seen on the statue's cheeks, lips, eyes, neck and chest. The statue was said to have wept a total of six times.

A DEVIL'S SPIRIT
1895
Lake Ncovi, Gabon, West Africa

The intrepid explorer, Mary Kingsley, was bathing alone in the lake when the saw a violet ball, the size of a small orange, coming towards her from the forest on the shore. It was joined by a second ball and they appeared to circle around each other. She followed the lights, but one disappeared into the bush and the other sank into the lake. Local natives believed the lights to be "aku", a devil's spirit.

THE GHOST OF WILFRED OWEN
November 1918
nr Victoria, South Africa

Harold Owen didn't feel like celebrating the armistice, he was too concerned about his brother, the poet Wilfred Owen, who was still serving on the Western Front. One night as he was going to his cabin on the *HMS Astraea* he saw his brother sitting on a chair in his khaki uniform. Wilfred smiled at him and then disappeared. Harold knew then that his brother was dead. He had indeed been killed on 4 November 1918, but his family had not heard the sad news until Armistice Day, 11 November.

THE CURSE OF THE FLYING DUTCHMAN
26 January 1923
The Cape of Good Hope, South Africa

A stubborn Dutch captain by the name of van Straaten refused to heed weather warnings and insisted on sailing around the Cape of Storms, now the Cape of Good Hope, in horrendous weather. The ship was lost in the storm, and legend has it that he was condemned for eternity to sail the seas. The appearance of his phantom ship is said to be a portent of doom and disaster. In another version the captain gambled with the devil on deck and lost, again doomed to sail for eternity. In yet another version a goddess appeared on deck, was treated shabbily by the crew and in revenge she doomed them to sail forever. Richard Wagner turned the legend into an opera, renamed the captain van Derdeeken, and had it that the captain could go ashore once every seven years to try and win redemption by claiming the hand of an unsullied maiden.

A phantom ship, believed to be the *Flying Dutchman*, was sighted off the Cape in 1923. Fourth Officer N K Stone said the ship was sighted at a quarter-past-midnight when a luminous light appeared in front of them. Gradually the men made out the shape of an old-fashioned ship steaming towards them at full speed. The Second Officer made the immortal comment "My God, Stone, it's a ghost ship". It was also sighted back in the

1880s when the future King George V was serving on a ship in the Cape. He noted simply in the ship's log that "the *Flying Dutchman* crossed our bows".

ROY'S DEATH FORESEEN
Early 1940s
RAF Base, Egypt

Commander George Potter and Flying Officer Reg Lamb spent an evening drinking in the officers mess with a Wing Commander, only known to posterity as 'Roy'. At one point, Potter looked towards Roy, who was laughing with a group of friends, and saw an image of Roy's head with no eyes, lips peeled back and his flesh a horrid greenish purple colour. Lamb asked what was wrong. Potter described the vision to Lamb, but his colleague couldn't see anything wrong. The following night Roy was shot down over the Mediterranean. Potter believed he had seen a premonition of Roy's corpse in the sea that night.

THE GHOSTLY PREGNANCY DETECTOR
1952
The Transkei, South Africa

At this time Margaret Leigh was doing occupational therapy work at a mission hospital, and she and her husband lived in a very simple cottage with a thatched roof and stone walls. Margaret began to feel rather broody whilst they were living there, but that was soon to be the least of their troubles. On one occasion there came a knock on the door, but when they answered it no one was there. This happened on several occasions and eventually the Leighs stopped answering the door. They would also hear a shuffling sound, as though someone with a limp was crossing the living room. The ghost would restlessly prowl from the couch to the cupboard in the room and then back again.

On talking to the locals they learnt that their ghost was called 'Cousin John' and he had stored his drinks in the cupboard, much to his wife's disapproval. When Margaret became pregnant towards the end of the year, the ghost's visits became even more regular, and unnerved many of their guests. When the child was born though, the haunting abruptly ceased, and soon afterwards the family returned to England. The Leighs re-visited the house a few years later, and heard from the current occupants that they were plagued by a ghost. Margaret guessed correctly that the woman was in the early stages of pregnancy. It appeared that, for reasons best known to himself 'Cousin John' liked to be around pregnant women.

THE VIRGIN MARY AT ZEITOUN
began 2 April 1968
Zeitoun, Cairo, Egypt

Late one night three Muslim mechanics sighted a vision of the Virgin Mary standing on top of St Mary's Coptic Church, in a suburb of Cairo. The apparition drew a considerable crowd and when they shouted, the figure acknowledged them by bowing and then rising skywards. This sighting was followed by numerous miracle cures taking place all over the city. For the next 14 months,the Virgin Mary was said to appear about two or three times a week. Sometimes she was around for only a minute, whilst on 8 June 1968 she lingered for about seven hours.

THE PHANTOM HITCH-HIKER OF SOUTH AFRICA

April 1978
Uniondale, nr Willowmore, South Africa

Corporal Dawie van Jaarsfeld drove for ten miles along a stretch of road with a girl hitch-hiker on the pillion of his motorbike. She was an attractive brunette wearing trousers and a blue top. He had given her a spare helmet and an ear-plug so that she could listen to the radio. However, when he stopped at the end of the journey, the girl had vanished, and the spare helmet was strapped to the bike. There have been sightings of the female phantom hitch-hiker on at least four other occasions. She is normally sighted around the month of April, and is believed to be Maria Charlotte Roux who was killed in a car-crash on 12 April 1968, at the age of 22.

THE SOWETO POLTERGEIST
10 May 1978
Orlando East, Soweto, South Africa

Inexplicable fires broke out at a house at Orlando East in the Transvaal, with an accompaniment of a shower of stones. The phenomena began on 10 May 1978, and furniture was wrecked and burnt in the process, whilst a number of windows were also broken.

THE NATAL STONE SHOWERS
July 1980
Pietermaritzburg, Natal, South Africa

Two adolescent boys were bombarded by stones which even continued in the boys bedroom, and only stopped when they finally left home. The phenomena was blamed on the local witch-doctor who had met the youngsters at a railway station, and had been offended at what he considered to be their insolent attitude.

THE KENYAN STONE SHOWERS
23 December 1982/83
Machakos, Kenya

A stone shower which started two days before Christmas 1982, disrupted the lives of the Kavoi family and lasted for six months. The stones, which often materialised out of nowhere, had everyone completely baffled. Sub-Chief William Ndunda was called to the scene and was hit by one. Nothing seemed to stop them, even prayers and personal visits by the local witch-doctor did nothing to alleviate the process. Like much poltergeist phenomena it had to cease of its own accord.

THE ZIMBABWE POLTERGEIST
1983
Warren Hills, nr Harare, Zimbabwe

Residents of houses in the Warren Hills believed that their homes were haunted by those buried in the graveyard beneath the buildings. A poltergeist epidemic broke out which produced stone showers resulting in many broken windows. The houses were also said to feel very cold, even on humid nights.

THE FIRE SPOOK OF REUNION
February 1983
St Pierre, Reunion

Here a 12 year old girl was responsible for several outbreaks of fire at the flat. The girl's clothes, mattress and bedlinen all inexplicably ignited. Surprisingly, for a poltergeist outbreak, this one caused lasting damage, for the flat was eventually completely gutted by fire.

THE NATAL POLTERGEIST

Christmas 1983

Pinetown, Natal, South Africa

On Christmas Eve loud crashing noises here, were heard at a house which continued right through the Christmas season. No damage was ever caused. It culminated on New Year's Day 1984 when 14-year-old Wendy Roos was startled by a very loud noise, as though a boulder had crashed on to the roof.

THE IVORY COAST BLOOD SPOOK

12 March 1985

Aboro, Abidjan, Ivory Coast

Blood spurted from the walls of a house at Aboro. Police and reporters were called to the scene and examined various objects caked in the stuff, including clothing, kitchen utensils, a shower unit and a door. The blood, which the residents said smelt foul, seemed to follow them around the building for every time they walked anywhere, their footsteps left behind traces of it. No one was injured or hurt during the impromptu blood shower.

THE KENYAN POLTERGEIST
22/23 July 1991
Thamara, Muthithi,
Murang'a, Kenya

The Muchoki family of Thamara village had their house burnt down, and the family claimed that the fire had been started by ghosts. The night before at 9.30 the roof had been pelted with stones after the family had gone to bed. As the family surveyed the burnt wreckage of their home the following morning, they were convinced that a supernatural agent had been at work.

Australia

THE PHANTOM SURGEONS
February 1941
Wearyan River, Northern Territory, Australia

Probably the most bizarre of all the cases in this book. A nursing sister was called to a remote area to help a man who had been shot in the leg, and whilst she was attending to her patient, two men arrived in white operating theatre gowns and gave her a helping hand. At the end she looked up to thank them, but they had vanished. Several aborigines also saw the mystery helpers.

LADY'S RETURN
1953
Sarina, Western Australia

William Courtney was mourning his greyhound 'Lady', whom he had just had to have destroyed. That night he heard footsteps pattering into his room and a noise like a heavy but soft object dropping to the floor beside his bed. He put on the light, fully expecting to see the dog, but there was nothing there.

THE STOCKTON HAUNTING
February 1970
Stockton, nr Newcastle, New South Wales, Australia

One of Australia's most compelling hauntings. Michael and Dianne Cooke fled their house at Stockton, near Newcastle, after a series of hair-raising occurrences. Their beds were found disturbed, toys were moved, a door knob shook loudly and their baby daughter was pulled upright by an unseen person. Friends who came to stay were also unnerved by the ghostly goings-on, but the Cookes had their story corroborated by the previous tenants who had also experienced some mysterious, and at times distressing, incidents at the haunted house. One recalled that he had been woken by somebody shaking his shoulder, another had woken up suddenly to find someone peering at him.

The couple suffered a very eventful fortnight before Michael Cooke had the experience that put the tin lid on things once and for all. He was walking outside when he chanced to look behind him and found that he was being watched by a white face with piercing green eyes staring out of the window. Michael candidly admitted that he became so uncontrollably scared that he felt tears rolling out of his eyes. The Cookes left their undesirable residence soon after.

THE MIN MIN LIGHTS
1981
Min Min, nr Boulia, Queensland, Australia

The Min Min Lights of western Queensland are one of the most famous examples of ghost lights on record. Named after a remote hotel and post office that once stood in the area near Boulia, a luminous ball of light has been seen on several occasions since the first recorded sighting in 1912. In 1981 Queensland Commissioner for Police, N W Bouer, received a report from Det. Sgt. Lyah Bowth who had witnessed the ball of light himself. He saw it at 1 o'clock in the morning, and watched it for five or six minutes before it dived towards the ground and was extinguished. He said it had started out as a bright white colour, but had then dimmed to yellow. This description of the legendary light has varied little over 70 years of sightings.

THE CURSE OF AYERS ROCK
1993
Ayers Rock, Alice Springs, Northern Territory, Australia

Frightened tourists from all over the world were claiming that Ayers Rock was cursed, with reports appearing in such diverse publications as *The Daily Telegraph*, *The New Scientist* and *The Wiccan* (the official newsletter of the Pagan Federation). Chips of rock are taken away as souvenirs but tourists have been returning them, and asking them to be replaced in their original positions. One tourist from Arizona claimed to have suffered nothing but ill-health since buying a piece of the rock. An Australian woman said she had suffered a still-birth and contracted diabetes. The Aborigines were baffled by all this, as although they believe their beloved Rock is sacred, they stress that it has no curse.

Even so, the Rock usually has a profound effect on many who visit it. At the height of the Dingo Baby Murder Case in the early 1980s, one young man, David Brett, gained considerable attention from the world's tabloid press when he announced that he knew for sure Baby Azaria had been a human sacrifice to the Rock, as he himself was cursed by it. He also believed that he was being hunted by members of an occult group intending to do evil to him. After his death, when he fell off Ayers Rock, his mother said that her son had told her he might be the victim of a ritual human sacrifice. The inquest ruled that David had died by accident, especially when it was learnt that he had suffered from mental illness for years beforehand. Something useful came out of his death though. His body was found lying near to baby Azaria's missing bloodstained matinee jacket.

South America

THE SAO PAULO STONE SHOWER
1959
Sao Paulo, Brazil

The stone shower started quietly enough one Sunday morning in April. Don Cid de Ulhoa Centro was reading his newspaper whilst his wife and the maid were preparing the lunch, and the three children were playing in the hallway. Suddenly Don Cid heard two loud thumps. When he went to investigate the children told him that someone had thrown stones at them. Several minutes later a whole torrent of stones began to rain down on Don Cid's hacienda, penetrating every room and bouncing off the walls. Don Cid called in his neighbours who were as baffled as he was. For the next 48 hours the stone showers continued at random, and crockery began to fly about the house of its own accord. Don Cid called in a priest, Father Henrique de Morais Matos, to perform an exorcism.

Initially Father Henrique conducted a small experiment. He placed an egg in the fridge. Very soon after an egg smashed against the wall of the butler's pantry. When Father Henrique opened the fridge, he found that the egg he had put there was missing. Three exorcisms failed to calm the phenomena completely, but it ceased after 40 days of its own accord. The catalyst was thought to be the maid, Francesca, who remained very calm throughout the ordeal and announced that she knew the phenomena wouldn't hurt her. Neighbours believed she possessed mediumistic powers. Francesca left the house soon after.

THE PHANTOM STREET
1960s
Haiti

Biologist Ivan T Sanderson was driving across Haiti with his wife and an assistant, when their car became stuck in some mud. They all got out and were forced to walk for many hours until they came across what seemed to be a Medieval French street. Sanderson said it looked Parisian. His wife saw exactly the same scene, but the assistant walked right through it without even noticing anything unusual. It was only when he stopped to offer the couple cigarettes that they noticed the street had vanished completely and they were once more in a remote location.

THE HAUNTED CAR
18/19 September 1960
nr Brasilia, Brazil

On this particular night a newly-married couple, the bridegroom's parents, their driver and Dr Olavo Trindade, a doctor, were driving along an isolated road from Brasilia to Belo Horizonte. The car began to show signs of overheating, but when they all stopped to investigate, nothing seemed to be wrong. Whilst they were looking at the car, they were pelted with stones. The driver fired shots from a gun, but the bombardment continued. The group decided to seek help at a nearby police station. The driver returned to the scene with a policeman, but this time when he tried to fire his gun, he found it had jammed. They switched the car headlights on to see if they could pick out a culprit in the glare, but no one was around in the isolated landscape.

The party set off again and the stone shower resumed and sand also began to blow into the car, even though all the windows were closed. The driver suddenly yelled that someone was trying to open the door. Dr Trindade leaned forward to hang onto it, but found that the door seemed to open however much he tried to hang on to it. The driver noticed a vague form outside the car window and everyone in the car began to pray loudly. They finally reached their hotel at 2 o'clock in the morning, and when the driver checked his gun he found it was now working properly. There wasn't a single scratch on the car. This is one of the most bizarre mysteries to come out of this vast and intriguing continent.

THE JABUTICABAL POLTERGEIST
December 1965/1966
Jabuticabal, Brazil

A very violent poltergeist outbreak, centring on an 11-year-old girl called Maria Jose Ferreira, and resulting in her death. It started amiably enough with the entity giving Maria flowers or sweets if she asked for them, but it wasn't long before it turned very nasty. There was the unusual phenomena of stones and eggs hurled around the house, objects appearing out of nowhere and crockery being smashed, but Maria was the victim of some evil ghostly practices as well. She was bitten and slapped, had furniture thrown at her, was nearly suffocated as she lay in bed at night when objects were found placed over her nose and mouth, was found to have no less than 55 needles rammed in her heel at one time, and her clothing caught fire.

Her family called in a Catholic priest to carry out an exorcism, but this only made matters worse, as objects began to fly about even more frequently. Maria was sent to a neighbour's house but the phenomena followed her, hurling stones at the girl wherever she went, but witnesses noticed that the stones appeared to have a magnetic effect on each other. Maria was taken to a Spiritist centre, where a medium communicated with the poltergeist. It said that Maria had been a witch in a previous existence and had caused much suffering and now it was her turn to suffer. Special prayers and appeals were offered to the entity, but the haunting continued. Maria's ordeal lasted a year, and ended in a tragic way when she was found dead through drinking insect repellent. She was barely 13.

THE IPIRANGA POLTERGEIST
1968 - 1973
Ipiranga, Sao Paulo, Brazil

A rich variety of phenomena was recorded in this case, including a stool sliding down a flight of stairs and through a closed door, rapping noises, a fire breaking out inside a bag of clothing and inside a closed wardrobe, clothing and flooring inexplicably soaked with water and then just as inexplicably dried out again, and objects were either moved or went missing of their own accord. The family tried moving house four times but were persistently dogged by the menace. Their ordeal only ended when their daughter got married, which probably meant that the poltergeist had lost its catalyst.

THE PHANTOM SHIP
1968
Isla de Chiloe, Chile

The Isla de Chiloe has been haunted for several years by a ghost ship called the *Calouche*. There were a number of sightings of it in 1968, but there have been many more at other times.

THE SUZANO FIRE SPOOK
1970
Suzano, Brazil

A typical example of a fire spook, which included an instance when a calendar hanging on a wall caught fire in front of a witness. A wardrobe was burnt and when the police were called they found themselves being the victims of inexplicable outbreaks of fire as well.

THE SOROCABA POLTERGEIST
began 18 July 1972
Sorocaba, nr Sao Paulo, Brazil

The home of Mr Fernando, Mrs Alda Riberio, and their six children, erupted with a poltergeist outbreak on 18 July 1972. Furniture was overturned, knocking broke out and a large motor tyre outside the house levitated. The haunting was investigated by a group from the Brazilian Institute for Psycho-Biophysical Research, who witnessed a heavy wooden shelf crashing to the floor. When the family sought relief at a neighbour's house, it was inevitable that the poltergeist went with them. When they returned home Alda was hit on the head with a flying brick, and one of the daughters was scalded with water from the kettle. Another of the girls, 12-year-old Yara, was thought to be the catalyst.

The poltergeist would only operate in daylight hours, and never after the lights had been put on in the evening. The family fled the house for good, and sought blissful anonymity, as nothing was ever heard of them again.

THE MATTO GROSSO POLTERGEIST
1973
Ponta Pora, Matto Grosso, Paraguay

Another case of poltergeist activity breaking out at a remote farm, where the family of Kerzo Okamoto were pelted with tomatoes, and stones rained down inside the house. A sceptical reporter, Kazunari Akaki, spent five days at the farm where he saw chocolates falling on his bedroom floor, noticed that his jeep had moved 40 yards without leaving a single mark in the soft mud outside the house, witnessed torches being thrown at the walls and found an iron railing lying across his bed. A fireball appeared which burnt damp clothing lying on a chair, and left an inch-wide scar on the family dog, who was sleeping nearby at the time. Burn marks also appeared on the thatched roof.

In May the ten-month-old baby, complete with pram, disappeared from inside the house and was found unharmed outside under a tree, yet although it was raining, the child was completely dry.

THE CARAPICUIBA STONE SHOWERS

September 1974

Carapicuiba, Brazil

Six slum houses were pelted for three weeks by stones, bricks and concrete, which appeared to fall out of a cloudless sky. Fortunately no one was ever hit by anything, which was just as well for the concrete was found to be so heavy it was difficult to lift.

THE HAUNTED JUNGLE
June 1978
Alto Anchicaya Dam, Columbia

An American Peace Corps worker, Craig Downer, was with a colleague at the Alto Anchicaya Dam when they both witnessed an unforgettable spectre. They described it as luminous, transparent, cloudlike, and whiteish with a greenish tint. It floated a short way above the ground, and was standing a mere 60 feet away from them. The two men were so unnerved that they ran back to their camp and found out later that there had once been a bad accident at the bridge which could well account for the peculiar spectre.

THE PHANTOM HITCH-HIKER OF PUERTO RICO
20 November 1982
The Chain', Mayaguez, Puerto Rico

Arabian businessman Abel Haiz Rassen was driving along a stretch of road between Mayaguez and Arecibo, known locally as 'The Chain', when he was flagged down by a man standing by the side of the road. Rassen agreed to take him as far as the El Nido restaurant, but the man, who looked about 35, made Rassen uneasy because he kept imploring him to pray for him. When he eventually pulled into the car park of the restaurant, people standing nearby noticed that Rassen appeared to be sitting in the car talking excitedly to himself. When someone dared to ask him if he was feeling alright, he indicated a passenger that wasn't there. Rassen had fallen victim to a phantom hitch-hiker! This particular one is believed to have been Valentin Carbo, who was killed in a car accident on 'The Chain' early in 1982.

THE SANTA FE POLTERGEIST
March 1984
Santa Fe, Argentina

As in a lot of poltergeist activity experienced all over the world, a house was bombarded with rocks and stones, but even more disturbing in this case was the fact that this was accompanied by screaming. Locked doors were also known to open of their own accord and somebody could be heard crying desperately "Mother! Mother!".

ITAPEVA'S STONE SHOWER
May 1987
Itapeva, Brazil

Rocks were plucked out of the soil and hurled at the houses by an invisible force, and one even fell through the cathedral roof.

Furniture and rubbish bins were also said to fly through the air of their own accord.

THE WEEPING VIRGINS OF PERU
1991
Callao, nr Lima, Peru

This tragic country, inflicted with national bankruptcy, earthquakes and a cholera epidemic, has also seen a mass of moving Virgin Marys. In one village alone, the port of Callao, tears shed from a privately-owned statue on 27 February, in another part of the village the Virgin shed tears on 1 May, and a few days later a statue just outside the village shed tears of blood. Shop clerk Luis Prieto summed up the whole situation, "we need a lot of miracles", he said.

BIBLIOGRAPHY

BLUNDELL, NIGEL AND BOAR, ROGER — The World's Greates Ghosts
Octopus Books (1984)

BORD, JANET AND COLIN — Modern Mysteries of Britain
Grafton Books (1987)

BORD, JANET AND COLIN — Modern Mysteries of the World
Grafton Books (1989)

CAMPBELL, JOHN L AND HALL, TREVOR H — Strange Things
Routledge and Kegan Paul (1968)

CANNING, JOHN (Editor) — Great Unsolved Mysteries
Weidenfeld Paperbacks (1984)

FORMAN, JOAN — Haunted Royal Homes
Jarrold (1987)

GUILEY, ROSEMARY ELLEN — The Encyclopedia of Witches and Witchcraft
Facts on File Ltd (1989)

GUILEY, ROSEMARY ELLEN — The Guiness Encyclopedia of Ghosts and Spirits
Guiness Publishing (1994)

HAPGOOD, SARAH — 500 British Ghosts and Hauntings
Foulsham (1993)

INNES, BRIAN (Editorial Director) — Ghosts
Orbis Publishing (1992 reprint)

MACKENZIE, ANDREW — The Seen and the Unseen
Weidenfeld and Nicholson (1987)

MACNAGHTEN, ANGUS — Haunted Berkshire
Countryside Books (1986)

NICHOLAS, MARGARET — The World's Greatest Psychics and Mystics
Octopus Books (1986)

PLAYFAIR, GUY LYON — This House is Haunted
Souvenir Press (1980)

PRICE, HARRY — The End of Borley Rectory
George Harrap and Co Ltd (1946)

PRICE, HARRY — Poltergeist!
Bracken Books (1993 reprint)

RANDLES, JENNY — Spontaneous Human Combustion
Bantam (1993)

RANDLES, JENNY AND HOUGH, PETER — Scary Stories: A Supernatural Year Book
Futura (1991)

ROBERTS, J. AELWYN — Holy Ghostbusters
Hale (1991)

SKELTON, ROBIN AND KOZOCARI, JEAN — A Witches Book of Ghosts and Exorcism
Robert Hale Ltd (1990)

SPENCER, JOHN AND ANNE — The Encyclopedia of Ghosts and Spirits
Headline Book Publishing Ltd (1992)

TABORI, PAUL AND UNDERWOOD, PETER — The Ghosts of Borley
David and Charles (1973)

UNDERWOOD, PETER — The A - Z of British Ghosts
Chancellor Press (1993 reprint)

WATERS, COLIN — Familiar Spirits: Sexual Hauntings Through the Ages
Hale (1993)

WILSON, COLIN — The Super Natural
Robinson Publishing Ltd (1991)

WOOD, ROBERT — The Widow of Borley
Gerald Duckworth and Co Ltd (1992)

I am also indebted to *The Fortean Times*, *The Psychic News* and *The Wiccan*.

INDEX

H

I

J

K

N

O

P

Q

R

S

T

U